How to be a

"Teenage girls today are bombarded with images from the media, music, and our society urging them to fit in and to "play the part". I so appreciate *How to be a Super Model*, because it not only speaks the truth of God's word, but Sheri lives what she talks about. In my 25 years of working with teenagers, and having a teenage daughter of my own, this is one of the best resources I know of to help them know the Super Model and be one."

- **Reed DeVries** - President of *First Priority of the Sioux Empire*, business owner, speaker

"Sheri (Riley) Prescott is an exceptional role model and is more than qualified to author a book for young women. Her life is a living epistle, which should be read by all. I have know her for her whole life and what she writes about she lives."

- **Cherry Meadows** - Vice President of *Crown Enterprises International Incorporated*

"To Mothers and Grandmothers of teenage girls everywhere: *How to be a Super Model* is a must-read for all the young ladies in your life! Sheri Prescott really "gets it". She understands the depths of the issues teenage girls face, and offers real answers founded on God's Word and His principles. After reading this book, every teenage girl will know just how beautiful she really is, and will understand how to find true love and fulfillment in life!"

- **Kelli Masters** - Miss Oklahoma 1997, Attorney at Law

"Sheri Prescott has those special qualities of compassion and concern that uniquely qualify her to address the issues in this book. She does so with a loving heart and her faith in the potential for good in every young person."

- **William B. Moody** - Past *National Chaplain Veterans of Foreign Wars.*

"As yōuth pastors we see a desperate need for Godly role models in this generation. Sheri has put into perspective what it really means to be a 'Super' model, working from the inside, out."

- **Rick and Brooke Plummer** - Youth Pastors, North Myrtle Beach, South Carolina

How to be a Super Model

Sheri Prescott

Printed in the United States of America

Publishing services by Selah Publishing Group, LLC, Indiana. The views expressed or implied in this work do not necessarily reflect those of Selah Publishing Group.

ISBN 1-58930-129-3
Library of Congress Control Number: 2004093169

Dedication

To my Dad and Mom, for always believing in me. Through your example and your love I have grown into a woman who desires to serve her Lord with every breath she takes. You are my mentors and I love you.

To my brother Willem, for challenging me to know why I believe what I believe. You are a treasure and I'm blessed to be your "big sis."

To my Grandparents, Uncles, Aunts, Cousins, and Prescott Family, thank you for surrounding me with God's goodness and joy.

To my sweet husband Tony, for loving me and showing me that divine fairytales really do come true. Thank you for your patience, faithfulness, and strength. You are my hero and I am so thankful to get to spend my life loving you.

To my precious daughter Savannah Rose. I am honored that God gave you to your daddy and I. You are our angel of joy, laughter, and peace. May you grow up to *know* Jesus, realizing that life in him is so much greater than anything this world holds.

Mostly, thank you Father for loving me un-conditionally and for entrusting me with your work. Life is meaningless without you; you are my everything!

Acknowledgements

My first book has been an adventure and a dream. I am grateful for all the help, thoughts, and wisdom I have received from countless teenage girls, close friends, and faithful mentors. This book represents every person who has shared with me his or her perspective on life. Thank you.

Sarah Zylstra, thank you for spending hours editing and re-editing my manuscript. Thank you for not laughing at my spelling mistakes and grammatical errors. Your dedication and encouragement was invaluable. You are an outstanding journalist and a truly dear friend.

Contents

What is a Super Model?

It all started one night when I was tucked in my bed, sound asleep, having sweet dreams. I woke up to a pitch-black room, with a glowing alarm clock that read 3:00AM. The two words "super model" came to my mind. I lay under my cozy comforter thinking, "OK, why on earth would I be thinking about supermodels? Have I been looking at too many magazines lately?" It only took me a minute or two before revelation hit me! I had been asking God to give me an idea to write a book for *you* about some of the things that He has been teaching me over the past 19 years of my life. Well, by the time this book is done, it will be over the past 25 years of my life. However, through reading and studying the pages in this book, you will figure out why the words "super model" have become so precious to me.

You and I may not be from the same town or from the same country for that matter. And we may not enjoy the same toppings on our pizza or flavor of ice cream, but we do have some things very much in common. We are facing trials and joys, thoughts and emotions, and some days that we wonder if we will make it through.

Today young women are dying from sex, suicide, and apathy. Our media and social outlets are doing all they can to paint a false picture of what life as a teenager should be like. From MTV to liberally slanted media and school curriculum, we are lost in an effort to be like the models of this world. We see the flashy covers of magazines and the divas in music videos and think these people have the keys to a wonderful life. We are deceived by this world's glitter and can't see far enough into our future to know that the only crown worth getting is from our Heavenly Father.

This book is not filled with do's and don'ts, rules, regulations, or religion. Nor is it the world's version of living a happy and healthy life. This book is not about lip-gloss or tank tops either. In each chapter we will tackle issues that are important to us as young women today. We will find out together that God has fresh and real answers to all our questions. These pages are a journey. Your journey and mine. A journey of growth, change, love, and purpose.

I am praying for you, my friend. I know that our Father has a very special and unique plan for your life. I am praying that my words will encourage you, challenge you, and motivate you down to your core! I believe that the Holy Spirit has something specific planned just for you. Something that will change and impact your life in a lightning rod kind of way! He is shaping you into the woman that he has predestined you to be from the foundations of the earth.

Being thirteen

When I was thirteen years old, my friends and I were looking through *Teen Magazine*, catching up on the latest styles, checking out the new gossip polls, and chatting about the teen models showcased throughout the glossy pages. We came upon the most hip make-up trends too. One said to wear dark brown eye shadow, another said sheer gold, and still another said frosty blue. It went on to say we needed to drink 3 glasses of orange juice a day to stay healthy, along with egg yolk face masks once a week for our skin to radiate a healthy glow. The funny thing is that we believed every word on those pages. After all, the magazine should know all the beauty secrets? Right? Wrong!

Now, don't misunderstand me. It's great to take care of the outside of your body. God gave it to you and expects you to protect and preserve it. There is nothing evil about being a model, putting on make-up, or trying to look your best. *It's all in our motives.* It is wonderful to take care of the outside of your body, but it is a million times more important to take care of the inside! Mind, soul, heart, and spirit! Being a super model in this case has nothing to do with our appearance.

Like me, you may have heard your grandma or another senior say, "It is more important to be beautiful on the inside than on the outside." I have heard it many times and it is finally sinking in. I used to think, "How could that be true when they don't put very ugly, overweight girls in movies?" or "Why do magazines have so many gorgeous women on their covers?" or "Why is it that pretty girls always get more attention?" I have learned today that beauty on the outside is very short-lived and over-rated. God showed me that his plan for my life is so much greater than anything this world could ever give me. (However, honestly I still struggle at times with these same issues. I think most females do.) With that said, there is nothing that even comes close to God's gifts for his girls! His desires for my life and yours are more wonderful than a million boys running after us, cover shots for glamour magazines, and CBS News calling every day to do interviews. Are you getting my drift?

In the world's eyes, who are the most beautiful women on the planet? Supermodels. You know, the ones that model for Victoria's Secret, Cosmopolitan, and Glamour. I guess you could also throw in the mix of singing divas and pretty actresses. They are this world's standard for beauty. Now, what should *our* standard for beauty be?

The night those words, super model, came into my mind, I believe the Holy Spirit was telling me that my standard needs to be a "SUPER MODEL" of Christ. A role model to the world of God's radical beauty on the earth.

What is a Super Model?

What does the word "super" mean? Webster's dictionary says that it is something excellent, a high grade of quality, something superior in status, and an excitement for life! What does the word "super" mean to you? *Philippians 4:8 says, "Finally brothers, whatever is true, whatever is noble, whatever is right, whatever is pure, whatever is lovely, whatever is admirable - if anything is excellent of praiseworthy - think on these things."* In another version it might say, "Think about what is super!"

Birthday gift

My parent's big green couch was a perfect place to sit and daydream about getting my ears pierced. I was so excited to have those little gold hearts shimmering from my ears. You see, my dad promised me that on my sixth birthday I could finally get them pierced and I was thrilled. Most of my first-grader friends had already gotten theirs pierced and I wanted to look grown up too. So on August 28th my mom and I drove down the road to the mall. I was smiling from ear to ear!

We pulled up into the mall parking lot and I threw off my seatbelt, darting for the entrance, dragging my mom behind. The next thing I knew I was sitting in a high back chair, trying not to cry because my new earrings made my ears hurt. It didn't matter though, I had my ears pierced and I wanted the world to know. It was "super" to me. A wonderful, super birthday gift!

Sometimes the most painful moments turn into the biggest blessings. We never know when God is going to give us a gift after we have endured the test. Can you think of a time in your life that you felt hopeless and hurting? Can you think of a time that God did something so totally cool for you that the pain was worth it?

Take a lesson from a lump of clay along side a riverbank. It looks so slimy and dull. It seems worthless. However, when a potter gathers it and puts it on his wheel, it begins to transform before our eyes. He molds, shapes, pushes, and pulls as the old lump of clay transforms into a beautiful vase. Because of the potter's patience and vision for the clay, something worthless becomes valuable. That's how we are! Our Heavenly Father is the Potter and we are the clay. He has a vision and purpose for our lives. Day by day he molds and shapes us into something more magnificent than any amount of money could afford to purchase. In God's gentle hands we are super, excellent, and of the highest quality!

Now that we know the meaning of "super," let's move on to "model."

A model is a representation of something, an example, pattern, and something worthy of being copied.

I think of three things when I hear the definition of the word model. First, I think of Jesus, whom I want to model my life after. Second, I think of having role models or mentors that I look up to, and third, I think of *being* a role model for someone else.

> "**Be imitators of God**, therefore, as dearly loved children and live a life of love, just as Christ loved us and gave himself up for us as a fragrant offering and sacrifice to God."
>
> EPHESIANS 5:1-2

Do you remember being in elementary school and thinking that the girls in junior high were so grown up? Once you get into junior high, you realize that it's not that big of a deal. We are always like that to some degree. In high school we think college women are so old. Then we move on to college and look forward to graduating, starting a career, or having a family. Every stage in life we see other woman that we look up to. It's natural.

When I was barely big enough to reach the sink in my parent's bathroom. I would strain to crawl up onto the counter to study how my mom put on her make-up. I thought that it was the most dazzling thing to put some of her moisture-rich, sparkling red lipstick on my lips too! I looked up to her. I wanted to be like her. She was one of my role models. My mom was someone worthy of being copied.

Now I look up to her beauty on the inside. I will tell you why in a later chapter.

You're the model

You are a model that someone is following today. Do you have younger siblings or cousins? What about younger students in your school or youth group? Many of them are modeling their actions and attitudes after your example.

> "Therefore since we are surrounded by such a great cloud of witnesses, let us throw off everything that hinders and the sin that so easily entangles, and let us run with perseverance the race marked out for us."
>
> HEBREWS 12:1

No matter who we are, there is someone looking up to us. Are we godly models of Christ or selfish models of the world?

Selfish, huh? I'm talking to myself on that one. There is not a day that goes by that I don't need to ask the Lord to give me a humble servant's heart and to forgive me for being selfish. My flesh wants to be selfish all the time! I want my own way and I don't want to think of other's needs before my own. How about you?

I feel ashamed when I look back a few years ago to when my mom had surgery. At the time I had just turned 16. My mom spent a week in the hospital recovering. I hated seeing her so pale and in pain. It hurt to watch her physical struggling. Just like she had been in the past, my mom was a pillar of strength and joy. She refused to live under her circumstances and spent each day thanking the Lord for healing her.

I, on the other hand, was doing the opposite. All I could think about was myself. How *I* was hurting by seeing her in pain, how *I* needed her to do things for me, and how *I* wanted my life to be normal again. By her second day home from the hospital I was complaining about picking up the slack around the house, vacuuming, and helping my brother with his homework while my mom rested. I thought, "Will I ever have my mom back or am I going to have to do everything around this house forever?" My attitude stunk and my mom knew it.

Thankfully, she did recover and I learned more about having a servant's heart. I learned that the world in "the Riley house" didn't just revolve around me. I learned that by taking my eyes off myself and looking for ways to bless my mom, I found great joy!

Don't hide your light

A super model is ... holy, obedient, surrendered, sold out, and abandoned to Christ! In this world we are the light. Let's let it shine! "*YOU* (that's you girlfriend!) *are the light of the world. A city on a hill cannot be hidden. Neither do people light a lamp and put it under a bowl. Instead they put it on its stand, and it gives light to everyone in the house. In the same way, let your light shine before men, that they may see your good deeds and worship your Father in heaven." Matthew 5:16*

Whenever you get school pictures taken or go to Sears for family portraits, you are under the light. Models in fashion magazines are under the same bright lights for hours each day. Sometimes the lights get so hot and bright that their eyes begin to see spots of light and dark, sometimes red everywhere.

As Christians, we are the light. Sometimes it is a great encouragement to other people and they are drawn to us because of it. Other times, we are like those dark spots because we remind them of the sin in their lives. They either steer clear of us or they persecute us for the light. It is a fact that being under the light or in our case, *being* the light isn't easy. Our Heavenly Father never said that it would be easy. Quite the contrary! He said that it *would* be hard and that we *will* want to give up. We will be persecuted, but through His strength we can endure.

> "In this godless world you will continue to experience difficulties. But, take heart! I've conquered the world."
>
> *John 16:33b The Message*

A woman was asked by her coworker, "What is it like to be a Christian?"

The woman replied, "It is like being a pumpkin. God picks you from the patch, brings you in, and washes all the dirt off you. Then He cuts off the top and scoops out all the yucky stuff. He removes the seeds of doubt, hate and greed. He carves you a new smiling face and puts His light in you to shine for all the world to see."

Graduation

After my high school graduation, I was so excited to come home after my reception and open the mounds of cards and gifts I received. I don't know about you, but the green stuff was top on my list! I really didn't particularly want anything but money. Well, I opened one package; and I saw a small book called *Dear Graduate - Letters of Wisdom from Charles Swindoll.* I love books, but at that moment I was not in the mood to sit down and dig in. I am embarrassed to say that it wasn't until almost one year later that I cracked the front cover.

I was going to be a guest speaker at a graduation and was looking for speaking materials. Not only did I read the first page, I couldn't put it down. The pages were filled with incredible wisdom. In the very first chapter Chuck says, "Life is a lot like a coin, you can spend it any way you wish, but you can only spend it once." He goes on to share *Matthew 6:33, "But seek first His kingdom and His righteousness; and all these things will be added to you."* He says, "If I am to seek first in my life God's kingdom and God's righteousness, then whatever else I do ought to relate to that goal: where I work, with whom I spend my time, the one I marry, or decision to remain single. Every decision I make ought to be filtered through the Matthew 6:33 filter: where I put my money, where and how I spend my money, what I buy, what I sell, what I give away."

That's a super model to the core, a young woman who filters every aspect of her life through Matthew 6:33. It is very hard not to filter our lives through other things: teen magazines, boyfriends, the latest trends, the approval of others, New Age books, or standards on TV and in movies. What filter are you living through?

1 Timothy 4:12

From the summer of my 14th year on this planet, the verse in the Bible that has spoken the most to me is *1 Timothy 4:12*. It goes like this, *"Do not let anyone look down on you because you are young, but set an example for the believers in speech, in life, in love, in faith, and in purity."* Set an example. Be a super model!

When I read over Timothy's words I feel the Holy Spirit challenging me to be set apart. Why don't you take a minute to memorize it right now? I have. You'll be so glad that you hid this verse in your heart.

Let's look at it a little closer. What does it mean not to let anyone look down on you because you are young? If you're reading this book, most likely you are a teenager. Not all of you, but most. If you asked an adult if you were young, they would most definitely say "yes!" It amazes me that God says that we (as young women) should be the ones to set the example for the rest of the believers. Logically, it would sound more believable if he would have said, "Do not let anyone look down on you because you are OLD, but set an example for the believers...." But it specifically says YOUNG! Our Father doesn't make mistakes, so it must be the truth.

Many individuals in our culture look at young people and say, 'Let them have fun. They will make a lot of mistakes.' 'Don't give them much responsibility.' 'They are extremely selfish at that age.' Often people aren't surprised when teenagers skip work, turn in late assignments, or get caught with drugs or alcohol. You get my point. The lies of the devil tell us the exact opposite of what God tells us we are. My dear sister, did you know that the word "teenager" is never even used in the Bible? Only words like, "young man, youth, or young woman." According to Webster's dictionary the word "teen" means grief, misery, or damage and the word "age" means a stage of life. So the teenage years are referred to as years of grief and misery. No thank you!

On the other hand, the word "young" means an early stage of life and the word "woman" means an adult female person or feminine in nature. I don't see anything miserable about that!

I strongly believe God never meant our young lives to be filled with misery. That was something the devil made up to hurt us. We are young and we are women. Sure, we are learning a lot about ourselves, and our changing bodies. We do sin. We always will during our time on earth. But we do not need to make mistakes the way the world expects. They have set such low standards for us. You and I should grow and mature spiritually, just like we grow and mature in age. It's simple. Satan is the one who tries to confuse us and make it complicated.

So - you are young. Set an example. God never meant that we couldn't have fun and enjoy our youth. In fact, being young and being a believer is the best way to live. The world is looking for *the party* in drugs, sex, movies, pride, and greed. As a young Christian we have Jesus living on the inside of us - we take the *BEST party* with us wherever we go!

Let's look at Tiffany, a fellow super model making right choices. She doesn't have to worry frantically about offending her parents or hiding her dirt from them. They trust her. They don't need to be anxious that Tiffany is making out with some guy in their basement or taking birth control pills behind their back. She wouldn't. She is setting a *pure* example! And, unlike three of the girls on her soccer team, she won't waste time worrying about failing her algebra exam. She is setting an *excellent* example for her unsaved teachers by studying for the exam and by doing her best. She isn't perfect, but she does have right priorities. Tiffany also has true peace. She doesn't worry about her future: college, marriage, war, disease, and the unknown. Tiffany is walking by faith.

Ask the Lord to clean your mind from the deception that you are just an immature and irresponsible teenager. The Bible says that is wrong. *You* are the one who is going to set the example for others through *your* speech, life, love, faith, and purity! *You* are on the high road, becoming a *super model* of Christ.

Our Father's Love

As a small girl in Sunday school, I remember singing the song "Jesus loves me." For most of us it's the first Christian song that we are taught by our parents or learn in church. "Jesus loves me this I know, for the Bible tells me so. Little ones to him belong, they are weak but he is strong. Yes, Jesus loves me! Yes, Jesus loves me! Yes, Jesus loves me! The Bible tells me so!" Can't you just hear that sweet familiar melody?

You and I have been told that God loves us and sometimes we believe it. But do we fully grasp the extent of his love? Not only did he send his Son Jesus to die for us because of his love, but he has made a way through his Spirit for us to *rest* in his love. When we are hurting, discouraged, or ashamed we can run up into our heavenly Daddy's arms and receive all the perfect love he has for us. When we are excited about school ending and summer starting, he wants us to run into his loving arms. When we feel confused about a decision, he wants us to run into his loving arms. When we have sinned and walked away from him, he wants us to make a U-turn back into his loving arms. When we feel like giving up on this life, he wants us to fall into his loving arms. Get the picture? He loves us so much that he wants to be a part of every moment of our lives!

Our Father knows everything about us and loves us just as we are. *"Indeed the very hairs of your head are numbered,"* Jesus said in Luke 12:7. You mean God even loves my hair? He sure does. He even loves it when we have a bad hair day! His love is un-conditional and complete.

We can never become the super models that he created us to be unless we start to understand our Father's love for us. In one of my journals a few years ago I wrote, "Just as a little baby in a crib cries out to be held by her father, so my soul cries out to be held in the loving arms of God."

Do you remember when you were a little girl with pigtails or braids in your hair? I remember during that time of my life, my earthly dad was one of my biggest heroes. I got so excited when he would sit on the floor and play dolls with me. Or fill up my Barbie swimming pool with water. I remember he had a silly mask he would put on and chase my brother and me around our living room, making us laugh until our bellies hurt! I remember him being all dressed up in his dark business suits with a shiny red tie, going out for a meeting. He was bigger than life and I thought he was perfect. Little did I know at the time that his love for me was just a shadow of the love that my heavenly Father has for me.

Maybe you wish you could have a good relationship with your earthly father. Maybe he's not around or maybe he's too busy to notice when you cry. It's unfortunate, but the way we feel about our dads on earth is often how we feel about our heavenly Dad. We view God as far away if our earthly father is far away. We think God will abandon us if we have been left alone. We view God as angry if our earthly father has a short fuse. We view God as uninvolved in our daily lives if our father is very passive and seems uninterested in us.

Mr. Frost

I was blessed to hear an evangelist who has a ministry and calling on his life to teach us about the Father's Love. His name is Jack Frost. Really! His name is Jack Frost! I had to laugh when I heard it, but I'm so glad that I went to hear him teach. (I was surprised to see he didn't have white hair or snowflake print clothing.) He taught that there are six father types: the performance oriented father, the passive father, the absentee father, the abusive father, the authoritarian father, and the good father.

Which father type is your dad? He may be more than one.

The performance oriented father

Shelly's dad sat at the kitchen table with his arms crossed as he read her report card. He looked at each subject and diligently studied each typed grade. After what seemed like an eternity he looked up and said, "Shelly these four A's are good, but the two B's are humiliating. Don't you know that only losers get anything less than A's on their report cards? Shelly, you won't amount to anything. You might as well give up all hope for college." Tears welled up in Shelly's eyes as she hung her head low in disgrace. She knew her dad's love for her was based on how she preformed. If she succeeded she felt his love. When she made mistakes, his love grew cold.

If your dad on earth is performance oriented, ask God to help you to realize that there is nothing you could ever do to lose his love. There is also nothing you could ever do to make him love you more. His love for you is filled to the brim and overflowing. Even if you prayed for six hours a day and fasted for 40 days, he wouldn't love you more. Even if you got straight A's, won the talent search, starred in your own movie, and looked like Miss America, his love for you wouldn't change. And if you have sinned and turned your back on him every year of your life until now, he wouldn't love you any less. His love is not based on how you perform.

The passive father

Gwen's dad was extremely busy working on their family farm. He left for the fields before sunrise and came home when it got dark. He was a quiet man and rarely joined in during family discussions. His mind was always on his crops, the bills, or hunting season.

Gwen tried to talk to him, but every time she tried she ended up feeling more alone and rejected. He was in the very same room she was, but not *really there*.

If your dad is passive like Gwen's, ask the Lord to help you to feel that he's close to you. Ask him to make himself real to you and to help your mind and heart know that he will never let you go. He loves to listen to you and wants to be involved in every moment of every day of your life.

The absentee father

Kim was born into a single parent home. Her misguided and irresponsible mother had given birth to her while she was still a teenager herself. Neither of them heard from Kim's biological father and Kim always wondered why. As a tiny baby what could she have done to push him away? Why didn't he love her enough to stay and work things out with her mom? Didn't he want to protect her, watch her grow up, and provide for her needs?

If your earthly dad has died or left you alone to be raised by only your mother, you may need to forgive him in your heart for leaving you. You might not even realize that because your dad left you, your relationship with the Father might be hindered. Deep inside you may be angry with God. It's all right to feel that way. Please realize that your heavenly Father will never leave. At this moment, let the loving grace of your heavenly Daddy fill that void that you feel from your dad's death or absence. Run into HIS arms and never be lonely again!

The Bible says that our Lord is, *"A Father to the fatherless..." Psalm 68:5*

The abusive father

Sydney lived in a half million dollar house that was full of darkness. Her father would come home from his law practice each evening and immediately start drinking alcohol. There were many nights that Sydney and her older sister lay under their covers crying, holding each other as their dad yelled violent curses at their mother. He would hit and smack her face with the back of his hands. The words he spoke filled his daughters with terror.

You may have an abusive father. He may physically or emotionally abuse you. Have you pictured God as a cop in the sky that will punish you or abuse you for every wrong thing you do? That is not how God is at all. He would never hurt you! His love for you, the blood of Jesus, and a robe of righteousness covers all the sins you have ever done or will ever do. Again, he would never hurt you.

You may wonder how a loving God could keep you in a situation like you're living in. The truth is that his will is never to let you be harmed. He wants you to be loved and cared for by your earthly dad. He is holding your dad accountable for all he has done. Judgment will come....

Ask the Lord to heal those wounds from your abusive father. Let God patch up those sores and broken places in your life.

The authoritarian father

Bobbie's dad was in the US Marines. He was a moral man, but ran his home like he ran his platoon. If something wasn't in its place he would make the children stand at attention and do push-ups as punishment. He expected to be treated as a commander, not as a daddy. There was no distinction between home life and work. His idea of affection was saying, "Good job." Never, "I love you."

Is your dad the authoritarian father or ALWAYS right? He may be trying to control you because he feels out of control. Sure, our parents are an authority over us and protection from God, but in some cases that can get out of control. We could end up living with more of a dictator that resembles Germany's former leader, Hitler, than a daddy. Please realize that God is not like that, my dear sister. He will not "crack a whip at you" or "dictate" in an angry way over your life. God loves you and wants a close relationship with you. He will use discipline at times, but only because of his deep love. If your earthly dad is an authoritarian father, ask God to let you see him as a loving and caring father. There is freedom in Christ! *"Now the Lord is the Spirit, and where the Spirit of the Lord is, there is FREEDOM!" 2 Corinthians 3:17*

My prayer for you, sister, is that you will start to see yourself as a daughter, not a slave or servant. A servant can only bring people to a master, but a daughter can bring people to a Daddy! Yes, we are servants of a holy and all-powerful King of Kings, but we are also his children.

I love my earthly dad with all my heart, but some times growing up I felt like he was the number two dad. The passive dad. It seemed like he was distant and didn't always know what to do with me. Sure, he loved me, but he didn't always know how to show it. It was hard for him to build a relationship with me because of the distant relationship he had with his own earthly father. Sometimes it seemed to me that he couldn't figure out how to just sit back and enjoy me. I felt like he wanted me around, but he wasn't always *there*. His mind was focused on other things like business, bills to pay, and church activities, even if he was in the same room with me. It caused me to resent him at times and to talk back when he had an opinion contrary to mine. I reasoned that he didn't have a right to tell me what to do if he didn't want to listen to me in the first place.

God has healed my dad of those patterns and actions (and forgave me for talking back and harboring bitterness), but it has taken prayer and time. Today my earthly dad, Scott, *knows* how to spend time with me. My dad loves to sit and have long talks with me. He is anything but passive! Through God's grace and my dad's obedience he has become an outstanding father that I love and respect more every single day. He is and always will be my hero. A true daddy that is showing me in new ways the unconditional love that God has for me.

There have been many days, even months of my life that I have felt like God is far away or passive though. Is he really listening? Does he care about my busy days and sleepless nights? Does he really want to be involved in every decision that I make? The answer is yes. A big yes! He is the perfect father! He listens to me *all* the time. He loves spending time with me!

If you could create a dad, the perfect dad, what would he be like? Would he be at all your basketball games? Would he give you a big hug even when you got a D on your report card? Would he be the kind of dad that you could tell all your deepest secrets and dreams to, knowing that he would never tell anyone? Would he be the kind of dad that told everyone at his job about what a fantastic and beautiful daughter he had? The truth is, that no matter how wonderful we could imagine a dad to be, our heavenly Father would be even more wonderful!

Your *Daddy God* knows everything about you; you were created in his image. You are his offspring that he wove together in your mother's womb. You are his child; his planned creation. He wants to lavish you with his love. You are a gift, you were planned, and you have a future! (Check out www.fatherslovelletter.com – it's a great web site on the Father's love.)

Abba Father

One of my favorite songs by Rebecca St. James is called "Abba." She sings these words:

"I'm feeling like the eagle that rises
Flies above the earth and its troubles
Oh yes he knows that there are valleys below
But under his wings there's a stronger power

Oh Father, you are my strength
On you I wait upon

You make the road rise up to meet me
You make the sun shine warm upon my face
The wind is at by back and the rain falls soft
God I lift you high - You are my Abba (Daddy)"

Our Daddy is our strength and because of his love for us, we can come boldly into his throne room. We can run up onto his lap and let him hold us, just as we would hold a priceless little child.

Have you seen the Robin Williams' movie "Hook?" It is a modern day version of "Peter Pan." In this movie Peter Pan grows up and becomes Peter Panning. He is a successful businessman that is more concerned with his work in the office than he is with his role at home as a dad. He neglects his son, daughter and wife. He has forgotten what true happiness is and instead is filled with vast emptiness.

After many years had passed, Peter decides to take a vacation with his family to his hometown in England. While he's there, through a series of events, Captain

Hook steals his two small children. The only chance he has of getting them back is to learn to fly again. If you remember the fairytale you will recall that Peter can fly when he thinks of his "happy thought." Throughout this movie Peter can not remember his happy thought and looks for it all over Never Never Land. He thinks it might be in old friends, silly foods, or wild games. Near the end of the movie he finally realizes that his true "happy thought" is his kids! They are the only thing that brings him real joy and happiness.

You are God's "happy thought." When he thinks about you, he's full of joy. It's hard to comprehend in our small human minds, but God never thinks a negative thought about us. All his thoughts for us are good. God loves us period. We are his "happy thoughts!"

One of the first guys that I had a crush on in high school was Nathan. I thought he was the cutest thing. He was good looking, great at basketball, and he loved God. Well, he *asked me out* one day after school and my little heart jumped for joy. We started going out, although we never went anywhere! At the time I thought I really liked him, but now I know it was infatuation. He was a very quiet and private guy and sometimes would go days without saying more than "hi" to me as we walked down the hallway at school. Our relationship never grew and we broke up pretty quickly.

My relationship with Nathan is a lot like we are with God sometimes. We don't get to know him because we never talk with him. We are too busy to spend quality time getting to know him and his awesome love. Soon we begin to feel far away from him and end up forgetting how much he truly does love us. The good news for us though, sister, is that God's love for us is consistent even if ours isn't.

A fresh start

Have you ever moved and started school in a new town? When you walk in the school building the first day no one knows anything about you. You're the new girl in town and that's it. You have no reputation and no past mistakes for anyone to remember. For that one and only day you could appear perfect to everyone. It's like being given a second chance, a fresh start. After a few weeks or months go by, though, people begin to see who you really are - whether good or bad. The guys know if they want to ask you out. The girls know if they want to invite you to their parties. The teachers know whether you are an A or C student. No matter how hard you try, people have an opinion about you in both positive and negative ways. They treat you well or badly based upon those opinions.

God is not like that. The first day of your life he knew everything about you and loved you perfectly. He knew every mistake you would ever make. He knew your gifts and talents as well as your areas of weakness. His opinion of you can never change with time. His love for you from the beginning has never and will never change based upon what you do or say or how you look. He is not that fickle friend who comes and goes with the weather. His love is not based on circumstances.

Over half of all babies born in the United States are raised without their earthly fathers. Their dads have left, don't care, or sometimes just don't know how to care. Maybe you live without a dad. It's lonely. You hurt and wonder why. You might have decided to put it all behind you and act like you don't care. You can pretend to be tough and strong. God feels your pain though. He wants you to know that there is no one on earth that could love you like he does.

Reality is that we are often times hurt by our fathers. They should be the ones who are protecting us and taking care of us. That's why their betrayal hurts the most. It's ok to have doubts and to even rage against God sometimes. We don't need to protect God from the tough questions. He is big enough to handle them. Maybe we won't get all the answers now, but that does not mean we should stop questioning or looking to his Word for a response. We won't be healed unless we are honest about the wound.

I pray that wherever you are at this moment you would lay down right now. I am serious. Just curl up on your bed, on that bean bag in the corner, or just on a blanket sitting on the floor. Turn on some soft worship music and let your Daddy God wrap his loving arms around you. He wants you to know his love! He wants you to feel his love with your heart and not just your head. He longs for you to be close to him.

Let's pray this simple prayer together. "Daddy, I just want to know how much you love me. I know that there is no earthly father, even if he's the best dad on earth, whose love can compare to your kind of love for me. You don't look at my faults; you look at me covered in the blood of Jesus, forgiven. I know that to get closer to you, I must receive that free gift of love that you have for me. Let me feel the love that you have had for me since the beginning that will never run out!"

Let's talk about *you*

Have you noticed that the thing you love to talk and think about the most is you? Sure, this can be a sin when we become selfish, not concerned with anyone or anything else. On the flip side, it is important to love who you are. God created you unlike anyone else on earth. He knew he would create you from the beginning of time. He took delight in creating you!

Look carefully at these next words of scripture from The Message translation,

> "Oh yes, you shaped me first inside then out; you formed me in my mother's womb. I thank you High God - you're breathtaking! Body and soul I am marvelously made! I worship in adoration - what a creation! You know me inside and out, you know every bone in my body; you know exactly

> how I was made, bit by bit, how I was sculpted from nothing into something. Like an open book, you watched me grow from conception to birth; all the stages of my life were spread out before you, the days of my life all prepared before I even lived one."
>
> Psalm 139:13-16

Girlfriend, you were made just like you are for a reason. God made you an original. You are one of a kind. There is not a single person that is just like you. He chose to make your eyes the deep blue or radiant green that they are. He chose to make you stop growing at 5 feet tall or 6 feet tall. He chose to give you blond hair or brown hair. He planned how long your nose would be and thought about each special curve that he would give your frame. He knew the sound of your voice and chose to give you those pretty toes. Seriously, he loved creating you. You are his masterpiece, his priceless treasure!

Have you ever taken an art class? Let's pretend that your art teacher gives you a project. Your assignment is to create the perfect looking young woman. You can use watercolor, chalk, acrylic paint, or just plain pencil. All you have to do is create your best and you'll get an A+. Pretty simple assignment! So, you sit down and think about the perfect looking girl in your mind.... Two weeks go by and you're done with your project. Now your teacher has each student in the class come to the front of the room to present their perfect looking young woman. One by one, students unveil their work. Then you present yours and just like the majority of your class, you get an A+! Good for you! Now, as you sit back down in your desk you begin to realize that each student's "perfect looking young woman" was different. They were all different shapes, sizes, colors, and textures. Some you thought were hideously ugly and others you thought were exceptionally gorgeous. We all have our own version of beauty. God does too. However, he looks at each one of his creations and says that they are "good." No matter what they may look like to other people or even to themselves, God created his perfect looking young woman in each of us. You are that perfect creation that he planned from the beginning of time. You are HIS work of art.

What if two guys in your class mocked you, saying, "Look at her ugly piece of work!" That happens a lot to God's work. I think what hurts him deeply is when his own priceless creations want to change themselves. They don't like what he planned to be beautiful; they want to look like another piece of his art work. We do that a lot, don't we? Not just with how we look, but with who we are! I know that I have. I have at times in my life wanted to be taller. I've wanted thicker hair. I've wanted another girl's body. I've wanted to weigh less or more. I've wanted clearer skin. I've wanted a different set of circumstances. What about you? Do you complain about the shape of your face and sometimes the shape of the rest of your body too? What about your personality? Your talents? Where you live? How much money you have? The kind of car you drive or the clothes you wear? What parents you were given or the country in which you were born?

One of my all time favorite books is called, "You Were Born an Original, Don't Die a Copy," by John L. Mason. Throughout the book John gives examples of why it is so important to be YOURSELF! Your heavenly Father created you with a specific purpose in mind and if you live your whole life trying to become something you're not, you will miss out on the incredibly awesome plan he has for you. It's the truth! John writes, "God created you for a specific purpose. He called you not to imitate someone else, but to become all that he wants you to be. Simply put - you were born an original, don't die a copy!"

Being an original is hard work. It's hard because everything around us is telling us to conform - from newspaper and magazine ads to television commercials and movie scripts. This starts from the time we are born. Many well-intentioned parents have unknowingly increased the pressure for their child to fit in. They want you to be invited to all the "right" birthday parties. They want you to be involved in the sports that the neighbors have their children participating in. If GAP jeans are the fashion for school clothes in the fall, many parents go into debt for their children to look like everyone else. It's sad because all that teaches children is to be clones. They don't realize it's happening, but it is. Sure, there are good things about being like your Christian friends, but certainly not being *just* like them.

One thing I admired about my small high school class of girls was that none of us tried to be exactly like the other. In fact, I think we enjoyed the differences. Most of us enjoyed sports, but to varying degrees. A few were basketball players, one was a singer, and one was mainly into shopping and guys. None of us had the same hairstyle and most of the time we were all wearing different kinds of clothes. A few were more sporty and natural, while others liked the make-up and dress-up clothing more. None of us ever tried to change the other. To this day we are all very different and yet accept each others differences wholeheartedly. Those differences make us each unique and special. Wouldn't it be boring if God created us all completely alike?

If you begin to love and celebrate the person God made you, your whole world will change. Your eyes will be opened to see that God had a very special purpose in mind when he created you! Maybe he created you to be a giver. You are the kind of person that makes everyone feel better just by listening to them. You don't have much to say, but the love in your eyes says it all. Possibly you are very outgoing, popular and very often you have an overwhelming influence on those around you. You are bubbly, happy, and loud! On the other hand, you may be a bit more reserved and your happiest moments are spent alone reading in your favorite chair. You are very intelligent and get superior ratings on all your test scores. And, I don't want to forget that you may be an individual who is filled with passion about an issue or two. You are not overly outgoing and friendly, but you affect change everywhere you go. You are a leader to the core.

Sometimes we have very good reasons for not liking who we are. If we are lying, harboring bitterness, or hurting someone else we have a good reason to be disappointed in ourselves. When we could have done our best and we just gave a situation 50% effort, we can be upset with who we have become. Apathy and mediocrity have a way of making us feel worthless. However, in those instances what we need to do is ask for forgiveness and make a 180-degree turn!

It seems like every time I turn on the television or even drive down the road I see pictures of the world's version of beauty. It's everywhere—from magazines in Target to movie covers in Blockbuster Video to Pepsi ads. It is so easy to look at someone else and wish I had something like them. That's when I need to take every thought captive and make it obedient to Christ. I force myself to remember that I am God's chosen creation, he loves me perfectly, and I am wonderfully made! Remember Psalm 139? Many times I repeat that part of the Word out loud! The Bible says that Satan has to flee when we command him to. I command him to leave my thoughts alone each day! Say these words out loud with me: "I am my Father's chosen creation, he loves me perfectly, and I am wonderfully made!" Don't you feel better?

You may have heard the name Heather Whitestone; she was Miss America 1995. Heather has a heart for the Lord and serves him faithfully. She is an excellent example of a super model! Heather has a lot to be thankful for, but she has also gone through many trials in her life. You see, Heather is deaf. She has never heard a bird sing or a rushing wind howl through the trees. I am sure that there have been times in her life that she has wished that she could be different than she is, but our God had and has such an amazing plan for Heather's life. He has shown her that what you and I may call a disability, in God's hands can be something marvelous. She can't hear the music that she dances to, yet she is an accomplished ballerina. At the Miss America Pageant when they announced her as the winner, she couldn't even hear those exciting words! Instead of complaining about what she doesn't have, she has become the best "Heather" that she can be. God has honored her obedience! She was made an original and has remained an original.

I believe in *you* sister! I believe that you have talents, gifts, and abilities that only you can bring to this earth! God has placed within you everything you need to know him and to make him known to the world! He loves you! He loves you just the way you are! You need to start loving *you* just the way you are!

The eaglet

One afternoon an adventurous Indian boy was walking through a dense forest. He stumbled across a thick bird's nest that had fallen out of the oak tree directly in front of him. He placed his tan brown hand inside the twigs and came out with an eagle egg. He had no idea what to do with it, so he put it into his smooth leather pouch on his shoulder and carried it home.

His parents had a brood of prairie chickens and the boy decided to place the eagle egg into one of their nests. He thought to himself, "Surely the mother prairie chickens would sit on this egg too?" After a few weeks the egg hatched alongside all the other baby prairie chickens. As the months went by, this little eaglet grew up learning to act and live like all of the prairie chickens around him. Prairie chickens don't fly. They eat bugs and small things crawling along the ground. They also make a lot of annoying noises. So, this little eagle learned to do the same things they did. He was trying to be just like them. He wanted to look like they looked and act like they acted. Yet deep inside he felt different.

On a crisp, cool morning after he was fully grown, the eagle looked up into the clear sky and saw the most amazing, magnificent, beautiful, powerful bird that he had ever seen. It was an eagle. He said to one of the prairie chickens beside him, "Wow! Wouldn't it be incredible to fly like that bird?" The prairie chicken simply said, "Sure, but you'll never be like him. You are just a prairie chicken like all of us. Your feet will stay planted in the dirt like mine."

Eventually the eagle grew tired of trying to be like everyone else around him. He realized that there is someone so much greater deep inside him. He had been so busy learning to be, act, and look like the prairie chickens that he ignored who he really was. One fateful day he decided that he had had enough. He was either going to learn to fly or die trying.

The determined eagle ran towards the side of a steep cliff, jumped, hurled through the air, and started falling fast! Within seconds his instincts caused him to open up his massive wings. He began to glide, then soar, and then fly just like that majestic eagle he had seen in the clear blue sky a few days earlier. He was now becoming who God had created *him* to be!

That little story reminds me of the many times I have tried to become just like the women around me or the women I see on magazine covers, forgetting who God created me to be.

Loving you like God does

I've heard it said that you can't really love other people until you love yourself. Jesus said in Matthew 19:19, *"Honor your father and mother and love your neighbor as yourself."* Don't you agree that it is pretty hard to hate yourself and at the same time love your neighbor? It's also hard to hate your circumstances and be happy for your neighbor's successes. It's so easy to get jealous of how Susan looks in her CK jeans or how Hillary spikes the volleyball with such force. When I am feeling bad about myself almost anyone's life looks better than mine. The Bible says that jealousy is sin.

> "You are still worldly. For since there is jealousy and quarreling among you, are you not worldly? Are you not acting like mere men?"
>
> *1 Corinthians 3:3*

We need to be content with who God made us. There is always something about who I am to be thankful for. Just like the little song goes, "Count your blessings name them one by one, count your blessings see what God has done...."

The saving blood of Jesus

After years of being abused by her father and several other men, Marjorie was suicidal. She had put everything good about herself in a lock-box stored away in her sunken heart. She threw away the key.

Many years later, the saving blood of Jesus washed her clean from 50 years of sorrow. One of the first things she did was give up that box in her heart filled with all those memories, situations, thoughts, and hatred. Her hatred was not just toward those men, but also toward herself. She had vowed that she would never love herself, that she was worthless.

She was encouraged by a spiritual mentor to sit down at her kitchen table and make a list of everything she could love about herself. Could she begin to see herself as God saw her? Marjorie said it took her over thirty minutes just to write down one. As she thought harder and searched her heart, the Holy Spirit helped her come up with over fifty things that she could honestly love about herself. That night Jesus set her free. He set her free from wanting to take her own life and replaced it with a new life! Life in him. She literally became a new woman! Maybe you need to make a list the way Marjorie did. Maybe you need to visually see in print the good in you, to see yourself the way God does.

No matter what sins you have committed or how far you have walked away from your heavenly Father, he still loves you. You are on his mind 24/7.

There are days that I cannot believe the Lord loves me and has a plan for my life. Satan tries hard to get me to wish I was someone else or had something someone else has. His whole goal is to make me fall into a miserable pit of discouragement. There are moments that his evil plans start to work on my heart and mind. What about you? Do you ever have those days? Days marked by unbelief and discouragement, maybe even days of wanting to take your own life when it seems too hard.

I have felt like I can try and try but I will never be good enough. I will never be good enough for my parents, for my husband, for my pastor, and for my Creator. Even in writing this book I have gone through times of wondering if it will ever be finished and published. I feel lost and hopeless. I quit thanking God for making me and I focus completely on my weaknesses. That is a dangerous place to be.

I think that's how Satan may have started to feel when he fell from heaven. He made the ultimate mistake. Instead of rejoicing and thanking God for making him the most beautiful among all the angels, he wanted the one thing he couldn't have. That one thing was to be like God. Satan may have become discouraged with who he was and thought his life of praising and worshiping God as chief among the angels was useless. Eve also might have felt that same way when she took the bite of fruit that sent our world into a downward spiral away from fellowship with our Father. Adam and Eve had everything! But the one thing they were told they couldn't have, they wanted.

Satan uses discouragement and fear to knock us down. He will use every device in the book to keep us there. Through the blood of Jesus we can stand up with our head held high, stomping that discouragement and fear to the ground.

The Goads, a music ministry made up of three handsome brothers and a gorgeous sister, sing a song entitled *The Man Who Walks by the Side of the Road*: "The man who walks by the side of the road turns himself around. He'll pick himself up and dust himself off, start all over again." No matter how many times you and I are knocked down, we can get up again. Let's leave it all at the foot of the cross.

My prayer for you and I is that we would begin to see how valuable *we* are! That we would rejoice in the beautiful creation of *us* that God has made. I pray that we would run from discouragement and turn our back to fear. I pray that we would not be like those whose sin of wanting to be something other than God created causes them to miss out on God's awesome plan. We are princesses of the Almighty King! We each have different gifts. We all look and act differently, but that's what makes up the body of Christ. As we fall in love with who God made us we are able to serve him through the gifts he has given us. You were born to be you! May you see that special gift every time you look in the mirror and start to thank God for the rare and priceless gift that is *you*!

What would you do if you were taking your new puppy for a walk and noticed a man dressed in a black ski mask? What if he were holding a gun in his right hand coming straight for you? Would you walk *toward* him or would you walk *away* from him? Most likely your answer would be like mine. I would not only walk away from him; I would *run* away from him!

Why is it that so many times we walk toward the things of this world? Why do we embrace the thoughts, words, and situations that could eventually kill us? They may not kill our physical body, but they will kill our inside! It all starts like a cancer. On the outside people with cancer can look healthy. They don't have blue noses or rashes on their cheeks. They don't have neon signs across their foreheads reading "cancer" in flashing lights. Cancer starts small, grows over time, and can eventually kill someone if not treated.

Our spiritual life is much the same. Sin starts small and over time grows to engulf the entire person if it's not dealt with. The Bible in 1 Corinthians 5:6 reminds us that a little yeast works through the whole batch of dough. It only takes one mistake to affect the rest of our lives.

> "Do not love the world or anything in the world. If anyone loves the world, the love of the Father is not in him. For everything in the world - the cravings of the sinful man, the lust of his eyes, and the boasting of what he has and does - comes not from the Father but from the world. The world and its desires pass away, but the man that does the will of God lives forever."
>
> *1 John 2:15-17*

One of my favorite Old Testament super models is a gal named Ruth. Her life was such an outstanding example to us that a whole book in the Bible tells just HER story! Ruth was a young woman whose husband, father-in-law, and brother-in-law had died. After mourning the deaths of so many of her family members, Naomi, Ruth's mother-in-law, decided that she wanted to move back to her homeland of Judah. At this point Ruth had a major decision to make. She could stay in her homeland of Moab with all the friends and family that she had grown up with or she could follow her mother-in-law into a land she had never known. At the time she made her decision to go with Naomi, Ruth believed she was going to a land where she would be destitute and rejected for her nationality. She had to choose between what was comfortable and familiar and that which was uncomfortable and scary. It was almost like she was moving from the USA to Africa. Big changes!

Naomi told Ruth that it was all right if she stayed in her homeland of Moab and Naomi wished her well. This is when Ruth courageously said,

> "Don't urge me to leave you or turn back from you. Where you go I will go, and where you stay I will stay. Your people will be my people and your God my God. Where you die I will die, and there I will be buried. May the Lord deal with me ever so severely, if anything but death separates you and me."
>
> *Ruth 1:16-17*

Ruth made a difficult choice to walk away from everything she knew. The Lord saw her obedience. He never misses a thing! He knew that it was hard for her to leave her old life and move to a world of unfamiliar people and customs. At that time she had no idea that because of her choice God would bless her far beyond anything she could have ever imagined. In that new land he gave her a husband, child, and family that she would have never dreamed possible. God made something beautiful out of her life.

At different times in our lives God asks us to walk away from something that we love in order to fulfill his plans for our lives. Once in a while he asks us to give up something easy like a new pair of Nike tennis shoes, but sometimes it is something much more difficult, like giving up a friend.

Association

There was one word that I heard over and over again from my dad while I was in junior high and high school. That one word is "association." All he had to do was look at me with a grin on his face and say that one word. I knew exactly what he meant. "Sheri, be careful whom you associate or hang out with, because you will become just like them!" He was reaffirming 1 Corinthians 15:33, *"Do not be misled: Bad company corrupts good morals."*

What kind of company do you keep? Are your friends building you up and encouraging you to live for Jesus? Are they lifting you up in prayer? Do the words that come out of their mouths bring glory to God? Are they consistent in who they are or do they act like Christians in church but at a school party you wouldn't even recognize them?

It is much easier to pull someone down than to pull someone up. If one 135-pound guy stood on a chair and another 135-pound guy stood on the ground, the guy on the ground has a much better chance of pulling the guy on the chair down to his level than the one on the chair has of pulling the other up. It's the same way with the friends that we choose. It is much easier for us to be influenced to get drunk if all our friends are consuming alcohol. It feels more natural to hate our parents if our friends say they hate theirs too. It doesn't make us feel as ashamed to drop out of high school if our friends are playing the losing game too. It is easier to give up on the hope of becoming a pilot if our friends shoot our dreams down with smothering words. Finally, it's much easier to be lukewarm in our faith if all our close friends are lukewarm too.

Who do you want to become?

I was 13 years old when I had a group of my girlfriends over one night for a sleepover. We spent the night laughing, eating Doritos, and watching girl movies. Around midnight, when my parents had gone to sleep, we got on the phone and called some junior high guys that were all staying together across town. I can't remember the exact words of our conversations with them, but I do know that I wouldn't have wanted my parents to hear! The conversation was about rotten music, making out, and lying to our parents about where we were going the next day. The Bible says to *"flee the evil desires of youth..."* (2 Timothy 2:22) and I know that we were *enjoying* the evil desires of our youth that night. We were not acting on anything, but we were talking about filth. Remember, the more you talk about garbage, the easier it is for you to start becoming garbage.

Little did I know, but around 12:30am my mom was awake, putting away some clean towels in the bathroom closet next to my room. She overheard some of the junk coming out of our mouths as we were on the phone with those guys. I can't image what she was thinking! The next afternoon after all my friends had gone home, she asked me to come downstairs into the family room to talk with her. I can remember it like it was yesterday. I plopped down on the couch and she sat quietly on a chair across the room. She began to tell me that she had heard the conversations that my friends and I were having the night before. (Oops, I was caught!) Tears started to stream down her face and the disappointment in her eyes was overwhelmingly convicting. Up until this point she was so proud of the young Christian woman I was becoming, but that day she felt like she was looking at a total stranger. It hurt her to see her daughter "being part of the crowd." She said a lot of things to me that afternoon. She reminded me that I was becoming just like the ones I was choosing to spend my time with. She reminded me that God had a call on my life and she believed I could be different than the friends I was with. She reminded me that she prayed for me all the time and longed for me to grow into a woman with a heart for Jesus.

My mom looked into my ashamed eyes and said, "Sheri, who do you want to become?" I thought to myself, "OK, Mom, you've gone crazy. I'm 13 years old and you're asking me who I want to become." She said it again, "Sheri, who do you want to become?" "What do you mean, Mom?" I kept repeating. Then it hit me. She wanted to know if my desire was to become just like the world around me or if I wanted to become like Jesus. She wanted to know if I was going to give my life to the Devil and his lies or if I was going to become a light in the darkness and walk in the Spirit. She wanted to know if I was going to let myself be pulled down by friends or if I was going to *walk away* from those relationships.

After my mom left me alone to think in the family room that day, I knew that something had to change. *I knew that I wanted to become like Jesus.* I knew the emptiness and pain I felt because of the sin in my life. I knew that the girls I was spending time with would just drag me down further and that I would end up exactly like them if something didn't change. I knelt down on that hard linoleum floor and *repented* that afternoon. I asked my Father to forgive me, to make me new. I asked him to wash me clean from all the filthy words that had come out of my mouth the night before. I asked him to give me the courage to walk away from the friends who were pulling me away from him. I wanted the strength that Ruth had to move into a new land and embrace God's best for her life. I wanted to step out of what was comfortable to me and choose to take the road less traveled.

Rick Warren says this in his book, The Purpose Driven Life: "We are products of our past, but we don't have to be prisoners of it. God's purpose is not limited by our past. He turned a murderer named Moses into a leader and a coward named Gideon into a courageous hero, and he can do amazing things with the rest of your life, too. God specializes in giving people a fresh start."

One of the hardest things to do is to walk away from a relationship that is hurting us. Believe me, I know! If our desire is to become a super model of Christ we must *run* away from "bad company."

Look into your past and see how you have become like the people you have spent the most time with. Sure, you may have completely different personalities, but your values and standards will be the same. It's similar to how basketball players tend to spend more time with other basketball players. Computer wizards tend to hang out with other computer wizards. Singers tend to hand out with singers and the list goes on and on. I encourage you to look at the people that you spend the most time with. Do you want to become like them? Do you admire how they honor their parents? Do you like the words that come out of their mouths? Do you want the attitude they have? The life they have? The goals they have? The relationship they have with their Heavenly Daddy?

Accountability

Do something radical and get an accountability partner to keep you in check! Someone who has a deep passion for Jesus and who knows the love of the Father. Someone who has dreams and goals for their future and isn't going to settle for less than God's best in their life! For me that person has been my mom. Many times I have asked her what she has thought of relationships that I have had. It's helped me to take a good look at myself and see who I will become in the future. Even now it's hard to choose friendships wisely. It doesn't get any easier with age. Now I have a husband who is my accountability partner as well as some solid sisters in Christ. I am thankful for their honesty.

Saying no to your comfort-zone

I love to put on my baggy sweatshirt and cotton sweatpants on a cold winter day. I love to make a cup of steamy hot chocolate and pile it up with tiny white marshmallows, curl up on my bed and read a book. It's so comfortable! However, there are times that it's not good to be comfortable. If I stayed on my bed I wouldn't develop any new relationships or have any new adventures. I would never experience the vast world beyond my four cream colored walls. Sure, I may never bump my head or slip and fall, but I would be stuck. Stagnant. I would probably get fat from all those marshmallows and loose all my muscle tone from never exercising. I don't want to live that way.

Heller Keller said, "Life is either a daring bold adventure or nothing at all." Our Father knows that it is easier to live life curled up with our hot cocoa, but he knows we will be missing out on far greater things! He wants us to grow and stretch. We can never become super models if we're always comfortable. Ruth certainly wasn't always comfortable; she didn't choose the easy way out.

My cousin John sent me an email that is an excellent example of growth.

There was a small redheaded, freckle-faced boy and his gray-haired grandpa who went on a hike one balmy summer afternoon. They came across a tightly woven cocoon of an emperor moth. They put it into a glass jar and the little boy took it home to his bedroom. He watched it for hours each day in wonder. Several weeks later he saw a tiny opening in the cocoon. He sat on the edge of his bed, anxiously watching this tiny insect work its way out. After a few minutes the moth quit moving! The little boy became frantic wondering if the moth was hurt or even dead. He decided to get a pair of scissors from his mother's sewing drawer and began to snip away at the cocoon. The moth emerged easily, but all it did was crawl along the floor. It had a big fat bloated body and tiny, tiny, shriveled up wings. The boy began to cry, shouting for his grandfather. The wise older man walked swiftly into his grandson's room. Gently, he explained that God created the moth to have to go through a struggle as it makes its way out of it cocoon. The pushing and pressure causes the fluid from its big, fat, bloated body into its wings so it can fly! In the little boy's kindness, he had actually wrecked God's plan for the moth. Through the struggle it *would have* become the lovely emperor moth that God had planned in advance for it to be.

It is hard to walk away from sin and go through the struggle of being uncomfortable. It hurts and it's not easy. But just like that moth, God has a special plan for each of his young women. He wants us to become everything beautiful that *he* created us to be. It can't happen unless we walk away from relationships that are hurting us.

Sister, get real with yourself today. Look at your relationships and ask your Father if those are the people that he wants you to be spending most of your time with. Even recently, through my husband's wisdom, God revealed to me a girlfriend of mine who was dragging me down emotionally and spiritually. She is allowing a strung out emotional roller-coaster to rule her life now. One day she is up HIGH and the next day she is down LOW. One moment she is on fire for God and ready to serve him wholeheartedly with her life and the next day she is completely negative, bitter, and only sees the hurt from her past. One day she loves me, the next day she won't even look at me. I love her but I know that I need to keep my distance. I pray for her and if she needs someone to lean on I will always be there in a time of crisis. However, as I look at the *daily* choices she makes in her life I know that I should have the courage to walk away. I don't want to become like her. I need to let her go and pray that she would run into the arms of her Father for help. *It is great to want to help our friends, but sometimes the best thing we can do is pray.* They have to make their own choices.

I believe in you! I know that no matter how difficult it may be, you *can* walk away from friends that are corrupting you spirit, soul, and body. *"I can do all things through Christ who gives me strength!" Philippians 4:13. You* can do all things through Christ!

My prayer for you is that our Father would give you courage like Ruth had to walk away. To go in *God's* direction with your life. No matter how hard it may be, the Holy Spirit will show you the relationships you need to let go. He will teach you to see his plans for your life so that the struggle won't be as hard. He loves you, sister, and has your best in mind! Decide to turn from your sin and receive forgiveness. It's a brand new day! You, my dear super model, will not let bad company corrupt the good morals God placed inside you. You are his!

Change hurts

Many years ago there was a humble young woman engaged to be married. Her fiancé was truly the man of her dreams and she was deeply in love. She could picture the life ahead of her and it filled her with excitement! She floated on air as she lovingly planned a beautiful wedding ceremony that would surround the couple with their dear family members and friends. It would be a celebration to remember! Then she and her knight would drift away into the sunset for a tender and romantic honeymoon. She also thought about their new home together and how she would make it a welcome place to live, laugh, and rest. Oh, how it thrilled her heart to imagine having babies together, raising them up to serve their Lord.

Her plans were sharply interrupted one afternoon. She found out that she was pregnant. She was pregnant and yet she was a virgin! Would her fiancé Joseph still marry her? What would it be like to carry the Son of the God of Israel? What if family and friends in their community found out? Would they stone her?

You guessed it. The young woman's name was Mary and she was chosen by God to carry his Son. Now sure, things worked out and an angel told Joseph that the Holy Spirit had caused Mary to conceive. She had not been unfaithful to her fiancé and she would still make a godly wife. It's easy to remember that Mary was blessed to deliver Jesus into this world. But can you imagine how much her life changed overnight? The Bible says in Luke that Mary was afraid at first. She was troubled in her spirit. The angel of God laid a lot on her at one time. The most amazing thing about the girl Mary is what she said right after the angel was done speaking. "I am the Lord's servant," Mary answered, "May it be to me as you have said." WOW! She wasn't thinking about herself, her needs, her fear, or her future. She accepted the Lord's plan for her life and was willing to change everything! More than that, she embraced the change. She was ready and willing to watch God work in her life.

The question I pose to you is, "Are you willing to change?" Our Father doesn't necessarily ask us to change something specific. We can still continue to play sports, have jobs after school, and spend time going to concerts with our youth groups. It's all about our heart attitude. Being willing to change our heart is a step on the road to spiritual maturity. There is not one great woman of God that didn't change.

Many of us are looking for a long list of do's and don'ts. This is because man looks at the outside, but God looks at the heart. We don't have to change a list of rules, but the attitudes of our hearts. As my parent's pastor, Shane Philpot, says, "We don't need twelve steps, just one." Jesus is that one step. With him anything is possible. By his blood and his passion for you, I am convinced that you can do anything!

Without change it's impossible to grow. Babies don't stay babies for long. They want to crawl, then walk, then run. During those stages of development they are growing. It's like when you look through a high school yearbook and read all the notes from friends. Many times they write statements like, "You're the greatest! Never change!" But come on, sister, who wants to be a high school senior the rest of her life?

One of my closest girlfriends is a steadfast example of being willing to change. She is not only willing, but she has begged God to change her. She desired God's best for her life. She knew that the woman she was wasn't who God had created her to be. Her journey to Christ is filled with many points where she got to see God at work, but it wasn't until she was in her 20's that she found the Savior waiting for her with open arms. Kelli gave her life to Christ several years ago and in just the short five years I have know her, I have seen the Spirit do miraculous things in her and through her.

Kelli and I met at the Miss America Pageant in Atlantic City, New Jersey - not the location that I would have expected to meet one of my best friends for life. She was Miss Oklahoma and I was Miss Iowa. I remember noticing a petite, beautiful, blond-haired girl sitting on the floor of the convention hall with her Bible open on her lap. I looked down at my lap and smiled because I was reading my Bible too. Throughout those 18 days at the Miss America pageant Kelli and I were able to develop a friendship that I know will last into eternity.

After competing in the Miss America Pageant, September of 1997, Kelli and I really didn't know a whole lot about each other. We each went back to our home states of Oklahoma and Iowa to fulfill our duties for the coming year. We kept in contact over the phone and through writing a couple of notes back and forth. I was able to make one trip down to Tulsa, Oklahoma, to visit her during that year. We stayed up all night talking, sharing, praying, and eating way too much Blue Bell ice cream! Kelli told me that when she gave her life to Christ, her father and mother didn't want anything to do with her. They thought she was involved in some kind of cult or had gone overboard with religion. They called themselves Christians, but they were far from knowing Jesus personally. Our God is faithful through trials and the Lord has filled the role of parents in her life. The Bible says in Psalm 68:5 that God is a father to the fatherless. He has also given her a new spiritual family to mentor her and show her how a godly home should operate.

Kelli's Savior is her very best friend, her source, and the one she leans on. She asked the Lord to change her into a new creation and use her life to serve him and to bring others into a relationship with Christ.

It's been a privilege for me to see her grow from a baby Christian into a mature godly woman of faith and power through the Holy Spirit.

Before Kelli became a Christian, people looked at her and may have thought she had it all together. She was a championship baton twirler, an articulate law student, and a Miss Oklahoma Pageant contestant with a bright future. However, on the inside she was completely empty until that day she came to the foot of the cross. She surrendered her life to Christ. She confessed him as Lord and believed in her heart that God raised him from the dead. She believed, confessed her sins, and was justified. She was saved!

Today my dear sister Kelli is even more beautiful on the inside than she is on the outside. Her life is a testimony of a young woman that God changed through his love and grace. Kelli is willing to give up everything to know the Lord. Her passion and goals have shifted from wanting success in this life to wanting success in the life to come. The earth has only temporary gifts, but the Father has given us a gift that will last for eternity. Kelli is a super model of Christ in this world, a godly example of being willing to change even when you have to give up what you thought was most important to you.

Fruit

Super models bear the fruits of the Spirit. We are all born with a sinful nature and need to be changed into the likeness of Christ. One of my favorite teachers in high school, Mrs. Hagen, used to ask us if we were bearing fruit. She taught us such a simple way of looking at ourselves to see if we were changing into the image of Christ. In fact, we can stay accountable with a friend by looking at each other in the context of Galatians 5:22,

> *"But the fruit of the Spirit is love, joy, peace, patience, kindness, goodness, gentleness, and self-control. Against such things there is no law."* It goes on to say, "*those who belong to Christ Jesus have crucified the sinful nature with its passions and desires. Since we live by the Spirit, let us keep in step with the Spirit.*"

Do you see those eight fruits present in your life? If we asked one of your friends or your parents what fruits they saw in you, what would they say? What would your teachers or coaches say?

Love

How much *true* love do you see in your life? I'm not talking about boy crazy, goofy girl talks. I'm talking about love for your parents, your siblings, and your friends. What about love and compassion for the lost? A love that burns in your heart for those in need?

One thing I respect about my parents is that they taught my brother and I to be quick to forgive and apologize to each other. We did have arguments, but for the most part we strove for a peaceful relationship. Don't we often treat total strangers with more patience, compassion, and love than we do our families? That's wrong. It's totally messed up, girl! Our goal should be to treat our parents and siblings better than anyone else. We should look for ways to lift them up and show them how much we love them. How about taking your little sister out for ice cream or just letting her hang out in your room and listen to music with you? How about writing your dad a letter thanking him for how he goes to work each day to provide for you to be able to take dance lessons or to go to a retreat? You could really surprise your entire family with a meal made especially for your older brother who's leaving for college next fall. Even frozen Stouffers Lasagna would be touching!

Do you hurt when those around you hurt? As I said before, does a love burn in your heart for those in need?

On a dark summer evening in Eastern Europe, I sat in a dorm room with my Hungarian friend Szilvi. I watched and prayed in my spirit as she told the life and love of Jesus to two lost souls. They were beautiful young women and the boys at our ministry camp liked to look at them. They wore tight shirts, short shorts, and a lustful look in their empty eyes. I didn't understand their entire conversation as the girls and Szilvi went back and forth in their native tongue. I watched as Szilvi went to the door of the room, opened it, and started knocking. She quoted Jesus' words in Luke 11:9 and 10,

> *"So I say to you: Ask and it will be given to you; seek and you will find; knock and the door will be opened to you. For everyone who asks receives; he who seeks finds; and to him who knocks, the door will be opened."*

The two girls didn't seem to understand so Szilvi repeated her words and actions. There was passion in her voice. A passion filled with love. I know they felt it. I know they couldn't understand, but they could feel. Can you feel for them? Can you love them?

Joy

Are you depressed all the time? Do you have a frown on your face where a smile should be? How much joy do you feel inside? Sure, there are times of pain and sorrow in this life, but the Bible clearly says, "The *joy* of the Lord is our strength!" Do you radiate joy? Do people feel lifted up when they are near you? Or are you like Eeor, the famous forlorn donkey in Winnie the Pooh cartoons? He always sees the rain cloud, never the rainbow.

Joy and happiness are two different things. We may not be happy about moving from our home in New York to California for our mom's new job transfer. We can still have joy. Joy comes from knowing that God is in control. Our world will change, but he will remain the same. God is still great!

> "Shout aloud and sing for joy, people of Zion, for great is the Holy One of Israel among you."
>
> *Isaiah 12:6*

We can choose to live under our circumstances or above them. By *choosing* to live under our circumstances we will hate living in California. We will make life miserable for our mom, and we will wallow in the depths of despair alone in our room. Or by *choosing* to live above our circumstances, we will look at California as a new adventure, a new place to explore with a new friend waiting around the corner.

Peace

How about peace? That's a good one to check yourself for right now. Our country has gone through so much pain and fear since September 11th, 2001. Satan has paralyzed many of God's people by suffocating them with fear. You and I *never* need to fear. We should choose to cast all our fear and burdens onto Jesus. He will carry the load. Our Father never meant for us to live in constant worry of what might happen to us or the ones we love. He longs for us to find the peace that passes all understanding!

My husband Tony is a soldier in the United States Army. He is currently stationed in Baghdad, Iraq, fighting in this war on terror. My flesh wants to worry about him. Negative thoughts come like a flood: Is Tony okay tonight? Could my loving husband be shot and hurting? What if he would get killed fighting for our freedom? What would happen to our baby daughter and me? How can I face another day without him? Lord, how could you let him leave me?

I cling to the words in 1 John 4:18 (The Message),

> "Well-formed love banishes fear. Since fear is crippling, a fearful life – fear of death, fear of judgment – is one not yet fully formed in love."

Because of Jesus "well-formed" love in me, I do not fear. I will not fear! I choose faith instead of fear. God loves Tony even more than I do. He knew even before we were born that my husband would go off to fight this war with the red, white, and blue beside him. We both face each day knowing that it's not in our hands. It in our Father's hands. Fear doesn't change our circumstances; it just allows Satan to have a foothold into our minds. Our spirits are renewed by faith...yours can be to!

More fruit

What about patience, kindness, gentleness, and self-control? It would take a whole other book just to talk about each fruit.

Stop! Stop right now! Take the time *right now* to write down what fruits you currently see in your life. Next write down the ones you don't see. Are you willing to change? Ask the Holy Spirit to give you discipline and wisdom. May you begin to manifest fruits in your life!

I love how Pricilla Evans Shirer writes about fruit in her book *A Jewel in His Crown*. She says, "I don't want to attend any pity party, especially one that is about me. Why? Because as God's chosen women, we should want others to see us moving about our lives with a noble bearing. They should wonder how we could walk with our heads lifted so high. Our goal should be to exhibit the fruit of the Spirit in such a way that others just want to come and take a bite out of us and experience the good taste of our lives."

Jesus talks about fruits in John 15.

> *"I am the true vine and my Father is the gardener. He cuts off every branch in me that bears no fruit, while every branch that does bear fruit he prunes so that it will be even more fruitful...Remain in me, and I will remain in you. No branch can bear fruit by itself; it must remain in the vine. Neither can you bear fruit unless you remain in me."*

The closer we get to Jesus, the more fruit we bear. And there are no limits on juicy fruit in Christ! We all have the same potential to bear fruit in all areas. As we grow in our relationship with the Father he will prune (or cut off) the branches that don't bear fruit. Pruning involves pain and change, but it's only for a season. I believe that it's always for a very specific reason. Jesus said that it would bring his Father glory if we bear *a lot* of fruit! We can only bear *a lot* by changing.

Bruce Wilkinson says in his book *Secrets of the Vine*, "In mature pruning (for us that's becoming super models of Christ), the pruning will intensify as God's shears cut closer to the core of who you are. God isn't trying to just *take away*; He's faithfully at work to *make room* to add strength, productivity, and spiritual power in your life. His goal is to bring you closer to the perfect and complete image of Christ." He goes on to say, "Tests of faith are various trials and hardships that invite you to surrender something of great value to God *even when you have every right not to*. You will feel assaulted or stretched by circumstances, but not distant from God; tried by Him, but not judged or guilty. A psalmist described the refining experience and the priceless results.

> *"For you, O God, tested us; You refined us like silver... But you brought us to a place of abundance."*
>
> PSALM 66:10, 12

Growing pains

Have you ever felt growing pains in your legs? I am only 5 feet and 3 inches tall, but I've even experienced them. Those lingering pains that move up and down our legs are for a purpose. Change and growth always hurt. There is no way to get around it. If you want to be a track star, you have to put in the time and miles on the track running. You get tired, you want to give up, but you keep going because you have a goal to cross the finish line in first place someday! A ballerina also goes through great times of pain as she learns how to balance in toe shoes. Her feet ache for days and her toes may bleed, but in her mind she can picture that lighted, packed auditorium where she will perform *Swan Lake*. The pain is worth it, and she is willing to change and grow to become a prima ballerina. The medical student is willing to spend hours and hours in books and research, dedicating years of her life to understanding the field of medicine. Although she must give up temporary thrills and step out of her comfort zone, she doesn't hesitate. Someday she will be sitting beside the bed of a patient she has helped to fight breast cancer. All those days and years of study will seem meaningless compared to the feeling she will have of reaching her goal, helping to find a cure for that horrible disease.

You can change, my sister. Even when it hurts—you can change. You can get out of the comfort zone that is holding you back from the call God has on your life! You can become a super model, a woman after God's own heart. You can give up that guy that is dragging you down. You can change that pride in your life into humility. You can make the time to get to know your Savior better. You can press on to win the prize when all the odds are against you! You can do it in Jesus' name!

Maybe you think there is nothing in your life that needs to change. If there isn't, you must be perfect. Hint, hint. Jesus was and is the only perfect person. If you are like me, you hate to see the sin in your own life. Some days it's easier to see the sin in others' lives and not your own.

It hurts me to see how far away I am from my Father when I let sin enter my life. Often I pray that God will show me my secret sins. He answers that prayer. He shows me when I have been selfish. He shows me when I seek after the spotlight or to be exalted in people's eyes. He also shows me when I have lusted after worldly things. He reminds me that I am a sinner saved by grace, who daily needs to be changed into the image of his Son.

Jesus tells us to change in Matthew 18:3,

> *"I tell you the truth, unless you change and become like little children, you will never enter the kingdom of heaven. Therefore, whoever humbles himself like this child is the greatest in the kingdom of heaven."*

What are little children like? Besides having chubby cheeks and adorable voices, they are loyal, trusting, pure, innocent, humble, joyful, and eager to be taught and changed! That's how we need to be, sister. When was the last time you asked God to make you like a child? It seems like we are so busy trying to grow up that we forget that our Father has called us to be like children.

One thing I love about spending time with kids is that they are always looking for ways to please me and make me notice them. When I was Miss Iowa they would color me pictures of crowns or they would sing me a funny song they learned in Sunday school. God wants us to be the same way with him. He wants us to live to please him because we love him and want to be noticed by him. His arms are open wide for bear hugs and his lap is always ready to be climbed into. He loves us and desires us to change and become like little children.

Tony and I were blessed with the birth of our first child this year. Savannah Rose Prescott came into our lives and we will never be the same. She is a priceless treasure, a miraculous gift. I see how often she loves to be held and rocked in my arms. I melt when I watch her smile at her daddy and reach up for him. Our Heavenly Father wants us to reach for him, to be held by him. He wants us to have that simple trust in him, like my daughter has in her daddy and me.

The small gate

2 Timothy 3:12 says, *"In fact, everyone who wants to live a godly life in Christ Jesus will be persecuted."* Our brother Timothy reminded us that we will struggle in this life and even be persecuted. Being a Christian should be like trying to swim upstream against a ferocious current of waves that are pushing us back. The world is swimming one direction and as super models we need to be swimming the opposite direction. It's like being an alien on the wrong planet. We can't understand the language and we don't like the food! We want to fit in, but it's impossible if we want to live for Christ.

Jesus challenges us,

> "Enter through the narrow gate. For wide is the gate and broad is the road that leads to destruction, and many enter through it. But small is the gate and narrow the road that leads to life, and only a few find it."
>
> Matthew 7:13 & 14

I am certain most girls do not find the road that leads to life because they don't want to change. It is so much easier to stay on that wide road with the rest of the traffic. Most of the world is traveling one direction and you and I are called to go the opposite way; to enter through the narrow gate. The world's cars are headed towards unbelief, suicide, anorexia, bulimia, sexual sins, drugs, cigarettes, homosexuality, and greed. Our cars should be going the opposite direction: towards peace, faith, wisdom, purity, selflessness, and love.

No matter what struggles you may go through in order to change, our God will give you strength! He will give you the strength to turn your car around. In fact, some of the other traffic will eventually turn around with you!

Just like the Holy Spirit gave Mary strength, gave Kelli strength, and gave millions of other teenage girls strength, he will do the same for you!

Let's pray this together, "Father I have sinned. I have tried to live an easy life, free of change. It hurts to change and to release the things I am holding onto. I want you to hold me on your lap. I want to go against the flow. I understand that by your strength I can do it, bearing fruit in all things! I don't need to be afraid of things I can't see. I am willing to go through fire now to come out as silver. I am excited to live a life that is continually changing to be more like you. I want to begin today so that you can use me to change the world tomorrow."

Your bouqet

A few weeks ago I broke my leg in a terrible moving accident. It was a compound fracture of both bones in my lower right leg. (You could see the bones sticking out of my leg!) The moment it happened I began to pray in a new language. My flesh was hurting more than I have ever hurt before. I was scared for an instant, but I laid my fear at Jesus feet. I knew that he had been wounded physically in deeper ways than I will ever be able to comprehend. He bore my pain on the cross 2000 years ago. Surely he would take care of me...Surely he would make me whole again....

After an ambulance ride I was wheeled on a stretcher into the ER. I required several hours of surgery for the doctors to put my leg back together. I spent five days in the hospital where God began to heal me. During those days I learned that accidents are a surprise to you and me, but not to our Heavenly Father.

He has made a way for us even before we know we need a way. We can't control our circumstances, but we can control our reaction to them. It's a chance to grow and to see in a fresh way the mercy and goodness our Father has for us. A chance to remember that we *need* him.

I received a special get-well card from a friend. The cover read like this, "From tiny buds come brilliant bouquets...." You and I may be small and feel as insignificant as a tiny flower bud. In God's hands, though, we are not insignificant. We may feel weak, unworthy, or undeserving. We may feel like we have sinned too much and been away too long. The truth is that God wants to help us grow from those fragile buds into brilliant bouquets, the kind that you see coming out of floral shops, rich with stunning color and fragrance. They are noticed because of their beauty. As super models we want to be noticed because of our beauty as well. Not a beauty based on our hairstyle or clothing choice, but a beauty that comes from the inside, spreading a glorious fragrance of God's goodness every place we go.

A young girl's dream

When I was six years old I visited Breckenridge, Colorado, with my parents who were attending a convention for their business. On the last night of the convention they had a very special guest speaker and entertainer named Cheryl Prewitt, Miss America 1980. My grandpa Bob had affectionately called me his "Miss

America" from the time I was a baby and my dad and mom thought that it would be fun for my brother and I to see her perform that evening. So with great anticipation we accompanied them to the convention hall. I can remember walking into a huge auditorium that boasted a large stage in the very center. The lights were blinding, but as my eyes focused I spotted one of the most beautiful women I had ever seen. She looked magical up on that immense stage, wearing a blue sparkling sequin gown. Her eyes sparkled even more than her gown. After she finished her first song, Cheryl invited all the children in the audience up on the stage for a special musical number. I still remember the words to the song entitled, "I Choose to Be Happy!" They went like this: "I choose to be happy, happy, happy. Happiness is a choice and I choose to be happy so I can be me! Happy so I can be me!"

That evening in the mountains of Colorado turned out to be one that would affect my young life in a dramatic way. Later that evening Cheryl did a book signing for her new autobiography and my parents purchased the book for me. I was a young girl, but a huge dream began to grow inside my heart. I dreamed of becoming Miss America someday, spreading the glorious fragrance of God's love to everyone I could reach.

Twelve years after I met Cheryl Prewitt, I was old enough to enter the Miss America Pageant system. I had watched the pageant year after year and had studied many of the former Miss Americas through books, magazines, and TV specials. You must be 17 - 24 years old to compete and when my Father gave me the green light, I went charging! More than the dream of wearing that shiny crown, my dream had become to make a difference in the lives of other young women. I knew that the crown would open up doors to get me into places I would have never been invited without it. The Lord had made it strikingly clear to me that this was his path for my life at that moment in time.

The pageant

In January of my senior year in high school I entered a local pageant in Iowa called the Miss Cedar Valley Pageant. The pageant was going to be held at the National Cattle Congress building (talk about small beginnings!), in Cedar Falls, Iowa. Local pageants are run just like the ones you see on TV, but they are a lot smaller. I chose a platform or community service issue called, "Empowering Youth to Excellence." My goal was to work with "Focus on the Family's" youth outreach programs and to talk to young people about morals, values, and making right life choices. I purchased my white interview suit, ordered my accompaniment track for talent, and picked out a fuchsia colored bathing suit. Everything began to fall into place and I arrived in Cedar Falls, Iowa, to compete in my first pageant.

I prayed for the Lord to use me for his glory. I told him that I only wanted to win if it was his perfect plan for my life. I wanted the judges and the audience to see his light shining through me. Nothing in life is worth having if it's not from him.

The day of the pageant went by so quickly that I can hardly remember it now. My private 12-minute interview with the judges went well and that evening I belted out my talent song, "For Future Generations," by 4 Him. "I won't bend and I won't break. I won't water down my faith. I must be a light for future generations!" Evening gown, swimsuit, and on-stage questions were over before I knew it and they were naming the second runner up, then the first runner up ... "and the new Miss Cedar Valley is contestant number five, Sheri Riley!" They brought me a bouquet of flowers and placed a small crown on my head. I waved triumphantly at my family and friends. It was a joyous moment! God had honored my faithfulness, hard work, and prayer. My mom always said, "Sheri, work as though it depends on you and pray as though it depends on God." That cold night in January, as I drifted off to sleep, I was no longer just Sheri Ann Riley. I had won a new title: "Miss Cedar Valley 1997."

The next three months I poured myself into preparing for the Miss Iowa Pageant that would take place the end of May. I woke up early in the morning while it was still dark to have my devotions and prayer time. (I am very thankful that I started forming that habit during my seventh grade year in school.) Then I would do my school work (I home-schooled the last few months of my senior year to be prepared for the pageant), do public appearances through radio and newspaper, speak at a school or youth group about values and peer pressure, practice my new talent song, and shop for interview suits, gowns, and swimsuits. I also did mock interviews and studied newspapers and books for possible interview questions.

The Lord used several people in my life during that time to help me realize my dream. One special lady, Becki Thompson, helped me create flyers for my *Empowering Youth to Excellence* platform. She also designed colorful stickers to leave behind with children to reinforce the message that I gave them. Another special woman was Marlys Popma, who directed me to Focus on the Family and helped me understand the Biblical worldview that I grew to hold in a deeper way than ever before.

I praise my Father that I remained focused on my goal during those months, letting nothing distract me. Jesus said in Luke 9:62, "*No one who puts his hand to the plow and looks back is fit for service in the kingdom of God.*" I realized that in order to achieve this dream, my priorities had to change. I gave up time with my family and friends, time spent enjoying the end of my senior year of high school, and time just sitting in front of the TV vegging out. I focused on the end result that I wanted and did not look back. What results do you want to see manifested in your life? Are you focused on those results?

The week before I left for the Miss Iowa Pageant I graduated from high school. I traveled with my family to Davenport, Iowa, for the weeklong Miss Iowa Scholarship Pageant. I was so excited! I realized three things about myself that day. I was one of the youngest contestants (I was 18), I was one of the shortest contestants (I'm 5'3"), and I was one of the least experienced in pageantry (I had only been in the Miss America system for 4 months). It was a little overwhelming to say the least.

Throughout that week all of us Miss Iowa hopefuls rehearsed for the production, spoke to the press, went to various luncheons, and had the preliminary competitions for evening gown, talent, swimsuit, and private and on-stage interviews.

As we rehearsed the evening gown production number I overheard several of the contestants talking about how much they had spent on their dresses. One said $800, another said $1000, and still another said in a snooty voice, "Well, my father spent over $1500 on my one-of-a-kind, beaded gown." She flipped her sandy-blond hair around and headed toward the stage. In that instant my heart sank and a lump filled my throat. We had spent less than $100 on my gown. In fact, I bought it at a consignment store, which is much like a garage sale.

I loved my white and gold beaded gown. I felt like a princess when I had it on, but the price made it pale in comparison with many of the others on that Alder Theater stage. I remembered the day a month earlier when I had my alterations done. The gown was too long. As I stood in front of the seamstress' full-length mirror, I told her how much we paid for it. I will never forget what she said in a heavy Spanish accent, "Sheri, it's the not the dress that wins. It's the girl in the dress." That proved to be true.

Toward the end of pageant week, I had my private interview with the judges. I confidently walked into an open room with six judges who began to fire questions at me for twelve minutes. Not fluffy, easy questions, but hard ones! Questions like, "Sheri, what do you think the gambling industry has done to the state of Iowa?" And, "Sheri, if your best friend was raped would you support her in having an abortion?"

I had been praying that the Holy Spirit would speak through me, and I knew that he would give me wisdom. My specific prayer was to speak with profound, intellectual words. I asked the Lord to shoot lightning bolts at the judges so they would know to pick me. OK, that was a bit much to ask for. As you may have guessed, there were no lightning bolts in the room that day. The interview went well. However, after I walked out of that room almost instantly my mind began to be filled with doubt and fear. Satan began to whisper in my ear, "Sheri, you're one of the youngest contestants. The only women who win state pageants are 23 or 24 years old. Don't you see how polished Tonya and Lisa are? You are the least experienced. The other girls know what they are doing because they have been in more pageants than you have. You are short! Only tall girls win pageants. You are also a Christian. Did you hear what you said in your interview? They are going to think you're a Bible-beater. You aren't politically correct enough." Tears began to stream down my cheeks. I went to the nearest pay phone to call my mom and dad.

I told my mom all the feelings that I was having. She tried to console me and remind me that I was there to simply glorify the Lord. It was all in his hands. Nothing she was saying was helping, though! I heard my sixteen-year-old brother, Will, grab the phone. He shouted, "Sheri, be quiet!" So I was quiet, more startled than anything. He went on to say, "Sheri, do you remember when Peter was walking out on the water to Jesus?" (See Matthew 14 for the story.) "Yes," I said, my voice cracking from fighting back the tears. "Well," Will said, "when he took his eyes off Jesus and began to look at the wind and waves around him, he began to sink. That's what you're doing, Sheri. You are taking your eyes off Jesus and your goal. You're looking at all the obstacles around you!" I don't know if I have ever been as thankful for my brother as I was that afternoon.

On Friday, before the final night of competition, I sat up late praying. I cried out to God as I hugged my pillow. I felt pressure on all sides. I wondered if I had really given my best, my all. I didn't want to let down all the people that had come to support me. I didn't want to disappoint myself, and most of all; I didn't want to disappoint God. I also really wanted to win. I read Philippians 3:14 which says, "*I press towards the prize for which God has called me heavenward in Christ Jesus.*" I made the decision to press on, knowing that God could use me to witness for him as Miss Iowa. I put all my fears and worries in His powerful hands and believed by faith that He had brought me there to win. I was going to keep my eyes on Jesus!

Saturday night

It was Saturday night and all of us contestants were in our dressing rooms curling our hair, putting on make-up, and getting dressed. The hairspray was thick and the duct tape out. The excitement was beyond belief as the curtain went up, the lights shone, and the music to the opening production number began to play.

They announced the top ten and yes! my name was called! I waved at my family and friends in the audience and felt energized by their wild cheers. Before I knew it we were done with most of the competitions and the judges were narrowing us down to five ladies and yes! my name was called again!

After our on-stage interviews were over, it was time to wait for the results. "Your fourth runner up is Miss Louisa County, your third runner up is Miss Heartland, your second runner up is Miss Greater Des Moines, your first runner up is Miss Johnson County, and yes - your new Miss Iowa 1997 is Miss Cedar Valley, Sheri Riley!" Thunderous cheers and a standing ovation began to roll through the auditorium as flowers were placed in my arms and a crown on my head. I began to thank the Lord out loud! Life was never going to be the same. I was rushed off stage to a TV interview, and then greeted everyone at a reception as the new Miss Iowa.

Sure, becoming Miss Iowa was a wonderful victory, but the struggles were hard. I wanted to give up many times, but I didn't because I knew that God had told me to finish. His plan and the blessings that followed were worth so much more than the nights of tears, hours of rehearsing, and the months of wondering if I could do it.

As I look back on my Miss Iowa year, I feel like God was taking a tiny flower bud, watering me, giving me shape, providing me sunshine, and carefully arranging me into a brilliant bouquet! He is doing the same for you. Each day that you put your trust in him, realizing your *need* for him, he is causing you to grow. He is giving you shelter and fashioning a crystal vase to showcase your beauty. You are rare and priceless, my dear friend. You are being prepared for this journey that has just begun.

Eat Right

How does a large pepperoni pizza with extra cheese sound to you? That's my very favorite food. Pizza is the best, especially the authentic Italian pizza Tony and I devoured during our stay in Venice, Italy, a few years ago.

I have a groovy idea, sister. Let's spend a day eating whatever we want. I mean *whatever* we want! These are going to be my food choices for the day. You can choose yours.

I'll start out with a large breakfast of ten crunchy strips of bacon, five eggs scrambled, homemade sourdough bread, butter, and raspberry jam. Let's add to that a tall glass of cold orange juice and a mug filled with chocolate milk. In fact, since I have time I'm going to indulge in a gigantic fresh baked blueberry muffin and chocolate chip pancakes with maple syrup too.

For lunch I'm headed to McDonalds for a super-sized value meal: a Big Mac, salty French fries, and a Coke! Next I'm going to drive across the street for dessert at the Dairy Queen. I'm going to have a medium order of cheddar cheese balls and an extra large strawberry shake. For an afternoon snack I think I'll just stick with a bag of Doritos, a sugary Mountain Dew, and a king-size Snickers bar.

Why don't you join me for dinner? We're having Kentucky Fried Chicken. A four piece, extra-crispy white meat meal for me! For my side dishes I choose macaroni salad, hot biscuits, hickory-baked beans, mashed potatoes, gravy, and creamed corn. I need something cold to wash it down. Let's see....how about a large Dr Pepper and regular milk? For dessert I'm craving two pieces of chocolate pie and a sliver of banana cream pie too. For an evening snack I'm going to order a Papa John's pepperoni pizza, of course! I will also need a can or two of Cherry Coke. To end the evening I'm going to have eight of my Grandma Ethel's delicious chewy chocolate chip cookies with a tall glass of cold milk.

Are you sick yet? I feel like throwing up! How healthy would it be for my body if I ate like that every day? I would probably weigh 400 lbs and be dead by the time I reach 30 years old. You may be wondering if you're still reading the right book. Don't worry, you are. However, this chapter is not about eating for our physical bodies, but it's all about eating the right food for our spiritual bodies.

What if I spent an entire day eating whatever I wanted to satisfy my sinful flesh? This is what I might do. I would begin the day with a morning talk show like The View for breakfast, followed by two or three filthy soap operas in the afternoon. I would buy at least one smutty fashion magazine a day and read Teen People each week. I would listen to Janet Jackson's music in my car and 'N SYNC would stay on in my bedroom all night long. In the evening I just couldn't miss "Friends," "Sex in the City," or my favorite dating reality shows. I would surf around the Net on sites that would make my parents skin crawl and my yahoo email would be: babyofyourdreams@yahoo.com. I would enter adult only chat sites, pretending I was 21, and scan pictures of myself to men I don't even know. I would spend hours on the phone in my bedroom gossiping about friends in my youth group and spreading rumors about what John and Molly did last weekend in the cab of his truck. I would fill my mind with teen romance novels and the latest horoscope predictions. MTV would be my favorite channel and Tom Cruise would be my spiritual guru.

Okay, okay! Now I really want to hurl! Seriously though, what if that was my spiritual diet? Is it yours? Maybe you are saying, "Sheri, that really is me. That's my life." I want you to know that you're not alone. Unfortunately, many Christian young women spend their time exactly as non-Christians do. Have you heard the saying, "Garbage in, garbage out?" That's the truth. If we put the lies and garbage of this world into our lives, that's exactly what we are going to get, garbage lives. If your spiritual diet is empty, how will you ever grow? You can't. It's impossible.

1 Peter 2:2 says,

> *"Like newborn babies, crave pure spiritual milk, so that by it you may grow up in your salvation, now that you have tasted that they Lord is good."*

We need to be hungry for the pure spiritual milk that God has for us. If we gave my baby daughter Budweiser beer in her sippy cup, she could get very ill. That thought seems outrageous, doesn't it? Why then do you think we can continue to put garbage into our lives and not become spiritually ill? We cannot be pure while living with filth.

A supermodel in the physical sense eats a certain way too. Do you think Tyra Banks, Cindy Crawford, and Heidi Klum have diets comprised of mainly junk food? Certainly not! It takes discipline to stay physically fit and appear in a swimsuit on the cover of Shape magazine. But it takes even more discipline to be in great spiritual shape. *"For physical training is of some value, but godliness has value for all things, holding promise for both the present and the life to come." 1 Timothy 4:8*

I do want to throw in a disclaimer that not all models eat the right diet. Many are dangerously thin, have eating disorders, and live a terrible lifestyle of roller coaster dieting. They certainly are not what we should be striving for physically. It is their concern with food that is what we should be emulating - but in the spiritual sense.

Running, lifting weights and playing tennis or basketball *are* good for us. The Bible says that they are of "some value." Being physically fit helps to keep our body (our temple) healthy. That's a very, very good thing. It's important. 3 John 2 says that John hoped that the Christians were enjoying good health. Eating food in moderate amounts is also very important. But nothing about our physical bodies is as important as our spiritual bodies.

So how do we go about eating for our spirits? Whenever someone starts a new diet or healthy eating plan, there are things they need to cut out of their old eating habits first. Some diet plans say to eliminate carbs, others say fats, and still others say sugar. It's not always so much a matter of what we eat, but what we don't eat! We need to check our portions!

Our spirits are full of garbage and are crying out for a good fast! "Fasting" just means going without for an amount of time. I have had many seasons of fasting so far in my life. During those days of going without, I drew closer to my Father and heard his voice more clearly.

Discipline yourself to do at least one of these fasts over the next week:

1. Fast from the television for one whole week, seven days. Don't even turn it on!

2. Fast from picking up or reading a fashion magazine for two weeks (like Teen, Cosmo, or Glamour.)

3. Fast from ALL secular music for one week.

4. Fast from entering ANY chat site on the Internet for two weeks.

5. Fast from going out to a movie or renting one for two weeks.

6. Fast from reading any romance novels or horror stories for a week.

7. Fast from playing any video games for two weeks.

8. Fast from talking back or arguing with your parents for two weeks.

9. Fast from flirting for one entire week.

10. Fast from the comfort you get from eating your favorite chocolate bar for one week.

I promise that after completing just one fast you will feel totally different inside. Why don't you go for the big time and try fasting from all ten vices for one whole month? It may sound like a lot, but I know you're up for it! Just by eliminating those habits from your life for a short time you will be on your way to becoming a super model. Be disciplined. You can do it! Fasting creates humility and the Word says that the Lord guides the humble and teaches them his ways. That's what we want! I'm not saying that watching TV or going to a movie is sin. In many cases it's not, but we have to look at our motives. Our portions may be off balance.

> "Paul and Barnabas appointed elders for them in each church and, with prayer and fasting, committed them to the Lord, in whom they had put their trust."
>
> *Acts 14:23*

You might ask, "OK, now what will I do with all my time during a fast?" I'm glad you asked. The next few pages are filled with delicious food groups to satisfy your growling stomach.

The Word

The very best way to eat the right, healthy foods is by consuming THE WORD OF GOD! The Bible! It's our #1 best food. For sure! Jesus said that man does not live by bread alone, but by every Word that comes from the mouth of the Lord. Our protein, carbs, sugar, fat, veggies, and vitamins are all rolled up into one power packed super-food. The WORD!

So, you just got done spending two hours at the AMC, eyes glued to a screen. Did you spend even two minutes in the Word?

Mike Murdock writes in his book *7 Keys to 1000 Times More:*

> "Your happiest days will be those days that you are *speaking* His Word to others, *memorizing* His Word, *reading* His Word, *listening* to His Word on cassette and *singing* His Word.

Everything you have always wanted is within His Word. *Everything*. Everything created was produced when He *spoke*. When he desired something - he spoke.

* His Word creates inner peace.
* His Word creates a climate of comfort.
* His Word warns of pitfalls.
* His Word purifies your mind.
* His Word changes your very nature."

The happiness Mike talks about can't be found in worldly foods. It can only be found through a hunger and thirst satisfied by God's words.

> "As the deer pants for streams of water, so my soul pants for you, O God."
> *Psalm 42:1*

In an article from Brio magazine (www.briomag.com), Jodi Carlson gives us some stellar reasons to dig into the Word. Jodi reminds us to pay attention, saying, "These are from God, so listen up!"

1. I love it when you pray. The stories in My Book will spark some cool conversations I want to have with you!
2. Get to know My disciples. Even though they lived thousands of years ago, they faced the same basic things you're facing!
3. When you read My Word, you'll naturally have more questions for Me. More questions mean more seeking. And more seeking means you and I are headed towards a stronger, more meaningful relationship.

4. I want your faith to be yours - not your parent's or your friends. Discover for yourself why you believe what you say you do.
5. My Son's love will come alive! You'll begin to see it everywhere you turn.
6. You'll be able to better advise your friends when they tell you about their struggles. You're My vessel. I want to use you.
7. Memorizing verses will remind you of My faithfulness. I never change and the promises in My Letter will see you through your changing circumstances.
8. Through learning about the disciples and other Bible characters, you'll begin to understand more about who you are.
9. When you feel distant from Me, reading My Word allows us to stay in touch and it gives Me a chance to draw you back.
10. You'll discover what My will is for your life.
11. When you're facing hard times, I offer you comfort here.
12. You'll grow intimate with Me - your very own Creator. Your Father. Your Savior. Your Best Friend.

As Jodi shared, we will grow intimate with our Father by spending time with him. We will better understand his plan for our lives. He will show us how to overcome our struggles by feasting off his Word!

The Bible says in 2 Timothy 3:16,

> "All scripture is God-breathed and is useful for teaching, rebuking, correcting and training in righteousness, so that the man of God may be thoroughly equipped for every good work."

The scriptures teach us everything we need to know to live, to serve our Father, and to grow into super models. It will rebuke us and correct us when we sin, fail, or are headed down the wrong path. It will train us in righteousness. The Word is our true food and nourishes us as we grow up by it. Jesus said that it will take more than hamburgers and French fries to keep us alive. *"It is written: 'Man does not live on bread alone, but on every word that comes from the mouth of God.'" Matthew 4:4*

Are you ready to answer?

When you are confronted by your science teacher on the subject of evolution, what do you do? Go directly to the *Word of God* and find out why they are wrong. Right in the very beginning of The Book in Genesis you have all the ammunition you need to prove that we didn't come from a hairy monkey. No, we were created in the very image of the King of Kings! *"In the beginning God created the heavens and the earth…Then God said, 'Let us make man in our own image, in our likeness…'" Genesis 1:1 and 26*

When a guidance counselor tells you that human life doesn't start until a baby is born and abortion is a woman's right, what do you say? God has given us his Word to prove that indeed life happens from the moment of conception, not birth. Jeremiah 1:5 is just one example,

> *"Before you were born I knew you, before you were born I set you apart…"*

Your politically correct friend may argue, "Homosexuality is not a sin. You're just born with it. Besides, Lisa is a lesbian and she's the most fun girl I know!" What do you say? Lovingly, share that God says homosexuality is a sin. No matter how much our culture wants us to accept it, it's still a sin. We should love the person, but we should not accept their *chosen* lifestyle. *"Do you not know that the wicked will not inherit the kingdom of God? Don't be deceived: Neither the sexually immoral, not idolaters, not male prostitutes, no homosexual offenders, not thieves, nor the greedy, not drunkards, nor slanderers nor swindlers will inherit the kingdom of God." 1 Corinthians 6: 9 and 10*

When you are confronted with witchcraft through a seemingly harmless board game, a weekly horoscope in *Seventeen Magazine*, or a tactful Psychic on late night TV, what should you do? Run! Then head for Galatians 5:19-21, *"The acts of the sinful nature are obvious: sexual immorality, impurity and debauchery; idolatry, witchcraft; hatred discord, jealousy, fits of rage, selfish ambition, dissensions, factions, and envy; drunkenness, orgies, and the like. I warn you, as I did before, that those who live like this will not inherit the kingdom of God."*

Those are just a few examples of issues you and I face. We need answers for those questions. The answers are clearly found in the Word of God. A clear stand is made! A line is drawn in the sand. No gray, just black and white. The problem is that you and I are floundering because we don't *know* what the Lord has to say on these topics. Have we gotten to know our Father well enough to know what he thinks? It's a frightening place to be, easily swaying with the world's views and opinions.

When we are eating from the Bible every day we will have an answer to the toughest questions the world throws at us. We won't be persuaded by other's opinions or by what our culture considers normal. The Truth shall set us free! *"You shall know the truth and the truth shall set you free!" John 8:32*

Today, start by opening the Word. Read. Pray for understanding. The Holy Spirit will make the stories and words come alive to you. You will lose track of time, wanting to read and read. Eat and eat! *"Teach me to do your will, for you are my God; may your good Spirit lead me on level ground." Psalm 143:8*

The Bible is our road map, sister. Whether we read our map in the morning, afternoon, or night isn't important. What is important is that we *use* the map! Be consistent!

I prefer to have my Bible study and prayer time in the morning before I start the rest of the day. When I had to be at school by 8:00AM, I would set my alarm 45 minutes before I knew I needed to get ready and leave. When I heard that loud buzzer, I would quickly turn it off (I don't like alarm clocks!) and switch on my little lamp. It was usually still dark outside as I quietly went into the kitchen to grab some water or milk. As I would walk back to my bedroom I knew that I was about to have the best time of my whole day and the day had barely begun! My Bible was always where I laid it the night before and my cat Mindy was up on my bed ready for devotions too. To this day that habit of morning devotions gives me the spiritual food I'm craving each day.

If you have a special time in the afternoon or evening to be in the Word, that's great too! Read any chance you get, in the lunchroom or on the bus! Any time is a great time to be in the Word.

A mentor of mine gave me a superb idea. She suggested copying a verse or two that really hit home to me that day on a note card. She told me to carry it in my purse or backpack, looking at it throughout my day. On several occasions by the time my sleepy head hit my fluffy pillow I had memorized part of the Bible that day. Cool, huh?

If your best friend ignored you one morning, how would you feel? I am talking about your closest girlfriend, the one you have shared your secrets with since kindergarten. Let's say she didn't talk to you or even look at you when you picked her up for school that morning. I don't know about you, girl, but I would be devastated. In the same way, if Jesus is really your best friend, how do you think he feels when you totally ignore him? You may go days, even weeks without talking to him, thinking about him, or getting to know him. Get the point?

Even now, after all these years as a follower of Christ, I still have days when I don't open my Bible. I feel embarrassed to tell you that, because it should be number #1 on my priority list 365 days out of the year! Not because I have to read, but because I hunger to.

I have repented so many times. I have realized that Jesus still loves me, forgives me, and wants to be my best friend all over again. It's like he's just sitting on the end of my bed waiting for me to grab his Word and enjoy all that he has done for me. He has forgiven me. Even when I fail as his best friend, he never fails as mine. He will never fail as yours either.

More food

Additional spiritual foods are books, devotionals, Christian magazines and study guides that you get at your church, Christian bookstore, or online. Books like the one you're reading right now! They are tools to help you along the way. One of my older and wiser friends says, "The only thing that will make you different five years from now are the books you read and the people you associate with." You will never grow if you don't read!

True friends

Along with that, spiritual food can be godly friendships. We become like those we hang out with. When we spend time praying with other believers in Bible studies, worshiping together at church, and talking about what God has done in our lives during youth group, we are eating delicious food!

Sharing the gospel

Eating spiritual food is glorious when we share the gospel. If you have ever led someone to Christ or have even just shared your testimony to plant a seed in someone's life, you know what I mean. We instantly grow when we do what Jesus has commanded us all to do every day. Be his witnesses! *"But in your hearts set apart Christ as Lord. Always be prepared to give an answer to everyone who asks you to give the reason for the hope you have. But do this with gentleness and respect. 1 Peter 3:15*

You and I are in full-time ministry 24/7. The Bible doesn't say we need to go to seminary or Bible college before we can minister to the lost. We are ministers already if we choose to be. Jesus said in Acts 1, *"But you will receive power when the Holy Spirit comes on you; and you will be my witnesses in Jerusalem, and in all Judea and Samaria, and to the ends of the earth."* The ends of the earth could be right in our back yards, in our school gymnasiums, and even in our own homes.

Music

Let's talk about Christian music. Or I should say, music with "Christian lyrics." One hot summer day I was driving down the interstate feeling sorry for myself. My day was not going the way I had planned. My husband and I had a stupid argument and I lost my favorite pair of earrings. I was complaining out loud to God.

As usual, I had my radio turned to the best Christian station around where I live, though I didn't notice it as I was having a pity party. The Holy Spirit knew what he was doing, though, and my ears began to hear the words coming out of those little car speakers. "Turn your eyes upon Jesus / Look full in his wonderful face /And the things of earth will grow strangely dim / In the light of his glory and grace." God was using a worship song to wake me up! I was so busy thinking about myself that I forgot my eyes needed to be on my Savior. Only then would the things of this earth (my silly complaints) become small because of his glory and grace. I was reminded that with Christ as my first priority, my complaints would fade into the distance.

We can turn on worship music in our bedrooms and be ushered right into the throne of grace. We don't have to be in a church building to worship. We can be anywhere!

Did you know music that glorifies the Lord wins battles? It can set us free!

> "As they began to sing and praise, the Lord set ambushes against the men of Ammon and Moab and Mount Seir who were invading Judah, and they were defeated."
> 2 Chronicles 20:22

What God did for the Israelites through music, he can do for you. The next time you are facing a battle in your life - crank up the praise and worship!

Stephanie is one of my dear younger sisters in the Lord. She's sixteen and beautiful inside and out. She has a passion to know her Father's heart. I got an email from her a few weeks ago in which she wrote, "Sheri, I desire to live for God while I am young because I know that he has a special plan and purpose for my life, and that I have to be willing to surrender everything totally and completely to him. I want him to be able to use me for his glory and not my own."

Stephanie goes on, "Last year at a Rebecca St. James concert after the altar call, she asked if anyone wanted to give their talents to God. I know that there are things that I want to do and be in life, but I want to do what God wants me to do. I want his plan for my life and not my own plans because I know that God's plans for my life are so much greater than my own. I know that I have to give up anything that is not pleasing to God, and humble myself before him. One of my favorite verses is 2 Chronicles 7:14, '*If my people who are called by my name will humble themselves and pray and seek my face and turn from their wicked ways, I will heal their lands.*' I have been praying lately asking God to show me what he wants me to do and be for him. I want to be faithful in the small things so he can make me ruler in the big things."

God used a Jesus-centered concert to help Stephanie realize some things about her relationship with Him. Through godly lyrics and music she was challenged to live a life worthy of the calling she has received!

Prayer

Are you full? Satisfied? I almost forgot one of the most important spiritual foods. We still have one more course to eat… It's called prayer. Jesus is recorded in the Bible praying more than he did anything else. He was consistently going off by himself to pray. He was also consistently teaching his disciples the importance of prayer. Jesus knew that the way to be closest to his Father was to talk to him and then listen to his voice. If prayer was that important to Jesus, don't you think it should be to us? We don't have to pray with fancy words, we just need to talk from our hearts. I talk to my Father the same way I am talking to you right now through this book. A baby cries out for its dad and mom when it needs something. We should cry out to God. If all we can think of to say is, "Help," he will rescue us every time.

"In the same way, the Spirit helps us in our weakness. We do not know what we ought to pray for, but the Spirit himself interceded for us with groans that words cannot express."
Romans 8:26

To keep yourself accountable to prayer, join a prayer group or set a specific time each day to pray with a friend or parent. The Bible says in Matthew 18:19 and 20,

"Again, I tell you that if two of you on earth agree about anything you ask for, it will be done for you by my Father in heaven. For where two or three come together in my name, there am I with them."

During the past 13 years, millions of young people have lifted voices, bent knees and joined hands to pray for their schools as part of **See You at the Pole - National Day of Student Prayer**, asking God to bring morals and spiritual awakening to their campuses and their nation.

In 2002, more than 2.5 million teenagers met for See You at the Pole in 50 states. Wow! I stood at my school's flagpole each September throughout my years in high school. I can promise you that I will never be the same. My peers and I stood hand in hand while we repented, made requests, and watched the Spirit of God move mightily in our generation.

Check out www.syatp.com for more information and to start or join a group of teens this September in prayer.

"And pray in the Spirit on all occasions with all kinds of prayers and requests. With this in mind, be alert and always keep on praying for all the saints."
Ephesians 6:18

I wrote this essay during high school for extra credit in English.

> *Then Jesus went with them to a garden called Gethsemane and told his disciples, "Stay here while I go over there and pray." Taking along Peter and two sons of Zebedee, he plunged into an agonizing sorrow. Then he said, "This sorrow is crushing my life out. Stay here and keep vigil with me."*
>
> *Going a little ahead, he fell on his face, praying, "My Father if there is any way, get me out of this. But please, not what I want. You, what do you want?"*
>
> *When he came back to his disciples, he found them sound asleep. He said to Peter, "Can't you stick it out with me a single hour? Stay alert; be in prayer so you don't wander into temptation without even knowing you are in danger. There is a part of you*

that is eager, ready for anything in God. There is another part that's lazy as an old dog sleeping by the fire."

He then left them a second time. Again he prayed, "My Father, if there is no other way than this, drinking this cup to the dregs, I'm ready. Do it your way."

When he came back, he again found them sound asleep. They simply couldn't keep their eyes open. This time he left them sleep on, and went back a third time to pray, going over the same ground one last time.

When he came back the next time, he said, "Are you going to sleep on and make a night of it? My time is up, the Son of Man is about to be handed over to the hand of sinners. Get up! Let's get going! My betrayer is here."

(The Message Translation. Matthew 26:36-46)

I have been thinking a lot about what Jesus is trying to tell me through this passage of scripture. We could focus on the terrible agony Jesus was going through at this time, preparing for the torture he would soon face. Or we could learn from his example of praying, "Let your will be done, Father." There are so many possibilities, but what I have been thinking about is his disciple's weakness of being tired and not praying even when Jesus urges them to so many times. He even scolds them for it.

I am like his disciples were that night. My heart wants to please the Lord in everything, but my flesh is weak. Satan tries his best to creep in and help me find excuses or simply to forget. I am sure that every Christian in the world has felt this way at some point in their lives.

We need to stay alert each day so that we do not fall. Peter couldn't stick it out for even one hour, no wonder very few of God's children on earth today can either.

Jesus comes to each of us and says, "Can't you just pray for one hour?" Or even half of an hour? Or even five minutes?" Why is it that so many things take that priority over prayer in our lives?

James said that the prayers of a righteous man are POWERFUL and EFFECTIVE! (James 5:16) Also, Paul reminds us in 1 Thessalonians 5:17 that we are to PRAY CONTINUOSLY! What a challenge!

Next time we spend an hour watching a movie, talking to friends, listening to music, playing sports, working, eating, or even helping out in a church activity we need to remember Jesus' own plea for us to pray.

If Jesus came to me today, would he say, "Sheri, are you still sleeping and resting? Why aren't you watching and praying?"

Daily we need to renew our minds and ask the Lord for his perfect strength to be men and women of prayer, especially in these last days. And as Paul pummeled his flesh to make it obey, so we need to do the same thing. Our life is not our own. We have been crucified with Christ!

"If my people, who are called by my name, will humble themselves and PRAY and seek my face and turn from their wicked ways, then will I hear from heaven and will forgive their sin and will heal their land." 2 Chronicles 7:1

To eat or not to eat

Prayer and Bible study go hand in hand. However, no one can make us do these things. Eating is our choice and must come from a hunger to know our Savior. It must come from our hearts.

When we pray we should talk to God just like we would talk to our best friend. Telling him everything! Then we need to be quiet. He will speak to us, remind us how much he loves us, and lead us in the incredible plans he has for our lives. He will be our Counselor.

> "… *And he will be called Wonderful Counselor, Mighty God, Everlasting Father, Prince of Peace.*"
>
> ISAIAH 9:6

So let's determine what we need to "fast" from, and start right now. Today is our day to begin eating the Word, fellowshipping with other believers, sharing the gospel with the lost, worshipping with thanksgiving and praise, and praying continuously. We won't find a better *diet plan* on earth!

Walk Right

Have you ever seen runway models on TV showing off the clothing trends for the latest season? They have a distinct and specific walk. They stand tall with their shoulders back, arms swinging at their sides. They might have a smile or just a blank, frosty look for the audience. Miss America pageant contestants also have a walk they must learn. Some girls even go to special modeling classes and schools to perfect their walk. Walking is of utmost importance to their careers.

What if a runway model was eating right, but not walking well? Can you imagine the pointing and laughter as she tripped and fell all over the stage? Her new nickname might be "Miss Clumsy." Most likely she wouldn't have a job for very long.

1 Peter 1: 6 & 7 say,

> "If we claim to have fellowship with him yet **walk** in darkness, we lie and do not live by the truth. But if we **walk** in the light, as he is in the light, we have fellowship with one another, and the blood of Jesus, his Son, purifies us from all sin."

Sometimes as believers our lives are referred to as our "Christian Walk." As we aspire to be like Christ, one of the keys is to *walk in the light* as we just read in 1 Peter. We can't have fellowship with our Savior if we're walking in darkness. Night and day are separated by darkness and light. They are totally different. Do your non-Christian friends know there is something different about you? Do your Christian friends see that you're walking in the light at church as well as at your school functions, dances, and sporting events? Again, we can't walk in the light and walk in the darkness at the same time. We can't have what this world says we need to make us happy and truly be happy. We need the truth of God's Word to shine a light into the dark places and make a path for us to walk on. *"The man of integrity walks securely, but he who takes crooked paths will be found out." Proverbs 10:9*

When I was seventeen years old, I left my country and headed to Europe for two months. I had prayerfully decided to go to Hungary and Romania for a second summer with a mission team called *International Messengers*. Our goal was to share the gospel through music, song, and drama across Eastern Europe. I was forever changed. God began to give me a heart for the lost souls of Eastern Europe. He got me out of my comfort zone and showed me He could change the world through my obedience! (Did you get that? God can change the world through our obedience.)

On July 5th I met the rest of the team of musicians from the United States. They became my closest friends for the next eight weeks. After hours flying over the ocean in a giant airplane, we arrived in Budapest, Hungary, where we joined up with the rest of our team. They were from Europe and El Salvador. Our unity was miraculous. Although we didn't speak the same languages or come from the same cultures, we were one in Christ.

My journal entry from day one

> Today is the very beginning. WOW! Father, it is so wonderful to be with everyone and meet each special person. I know you have so many wonderful things in store for this mission trip. Please teach me to be a servant, Lord. I really want to reach out to each person and show YOUR love through me. Please mold me and work miracles inside me! I so much want to be like you, Lord. Give me encouraging words for all my brothers and sisters and let your light in me shine huge! You are all I need and all I want. Make me yours! Father, I also want you to know again that I will do, say, and go anywhere you want me. I'm yours!

That summer was a grand adventure that I will never forget. From eating salami and cucumber open-faced sandwiches every morning to being stranded somewhere in the mountains of Romania when our bus broke down, there was never a dull moment. We had concerts in town squares, experienced unwelcoming glares, and even heard men yell for us to leave their land! Some days we could feel the spiritual warfare like a dense fog surrounding us. Other days our eyes were filled with tears as we saw weeping faces and broken hearts coming forward at the altar calls to accept Jesus as their Lord and Savior.

Another journal entry from later that summer

It is now 10:50PM and Rosita and I are staying at a new host home with a very old widow woman. She has given us so much delicious food that we could have hosted a party with fifteen others! She was so generous and loving. I sure wish we could understand what she is saying to us. Oh, well, it's fun to do mimes and try to figure out what the other person is trying to say. Lots of smiles too! And, one very funny thing happened too. She gave us some of the strongest coffee (Grandma Ethel would have loved it!) and when she turned around to do something, I poured TONS of sugar in it and tried to gulp it down fast. Gross! On another subject, our concert was really awesome tonight in a tiny little church. I sang several solos and they went great! Lord, I praise you for blessing me with a beautiful voice. Please let me never forget to keep using it to bring glory to Your Name!

Journal continued... It's now about 8:30AM and Lee, Roberts, Scott, Rosita, Szilvi, Edwardo, and I are back in the church. We are packing things up and waiting for the other team members to arrive. I just had to write really quickly about how much

I saw YOU in the old woman we stayed with last night. This morning she made us a lovely breakfast to feed an army again! Then she came into our room and saw the gifts that we had left her on our beds. She cried and cried. I wanted to give her so much more, but I didn't have much room left in my suitcase to bring many gifts for our host families. Then she packed us HUGE lunches and gave us each a quart of orange juice. WOW! Next she went to her china cabinet and got out two beautiful, intricately painted china cups and saucers. I wanted to cry, but I just hugged her close and tried to show her how much I loved and appreciated all she had done for Rosita and me. Then she prayed over us in Hungarian. I felt so cared for even though I couldn't understand her words. Lord, I learned so much about what being a servant really means. I saw Jesus so brightly through that old woman. Please give me some of what she has. I want people to leave me feeling the same way I felt about leaving her. But, I can't wait to see her in heaven some day... we will be able to understand each other then!

That summer in Hungary an old woman gave Rosita and me all she had. She was walking the walk! She showed us Jesus in one of the clearest ways I have ever seen. She was his hands and his feet. Her whole heart and attitude was to serve. I am looking forward to joining her in glory. I have a hug and a thank you for her. She showed me what a servant is.

"Whoever wants to become great among you must be your servant."
Matthew 20:26

Have you pondered the idea of going on a short-term mission trip? Or maybe you have already felt the call and gone. Either way, while we are young is one of the best times to step out by faith and GO. There is nothing holding you back and God is ready to do something radical in you, girl! Right now I have two special, beautiful, and godly girl friends, Brooke and Szilvi, who are in full-time ministry. They started by going on summer mission trips to Eastern Europe and now they are both missionaries! It's amazing to see how the Lord plants seeds inside of us and then waters them in hundreds of small ways to make them grow! I encourage you, sister, to step out and do something different next summer. Get online and check out International Messengers, Y-WAM, Brio & Breakaway Mission trips, or Teen Mania Ministries. Just think, next summer you may be in Africa, Europe, or Asia!

> "Passing along the beach of the Lake Galilee, he saw Simon and his brother Andrew net-fishing. Fishing was their regular work. Jesus said to them, 'Come with me. I'll make a new kind of fisherman out of you. I'll show you how to catch men and women instead of perch and bass.' They didn't ask questions. They dropped their nets and followed."
>
> *Mark 1: 16 & 17 The Message*

Jesus' disciples had to trust him when he asked them to start fishing for men. Did you notice that they didn't ask a million questions? They just started fishing. They didn't ask, "Why should we go?" "Will it be safe?" "Will I like this new kind of fishing?" "Where will my money come from?" Nope, they didn't ask questions. They dropped their nets and followed their Savior. That's what we are to do as super models. We are fishers of men and we need to start fishing!

If I hired a camera crew to follow you around for one week with a video camera, what would I see when I played your movie back? Would you be resting on the beach or would you be fishing?

Reputation

I don't know much about Britney Spears, but I do know that her words don't line up with her actions. She is a gorgeous girl and a wonderful singer and dancer, but that doesn't make her a good role model. When I see young girls dressing like her and singing her songs, it makes me sad. Did you know that you can still look beautiful and attractive without showing off your breasts and stomach? You can be a *star* without compromising your moral beliefs. Or you may have to give up your dream of being a *star* if it is causing you to compromise your beliefs. You don't have to dress half-naked and slutty for guys to like you. It's one thing to say you're a virgin and that you're waiting for your mate, but then you need to act like it! Don't lie when your actions (dancing, talking, and dressing) clearly reveal someone who has been sexually active. Only God knows our hearts, but our reputations and our testimonies are of utmost importance to our Christian walk.

> "A sterling reputation is better than striking it rich..."
>
> Proverbs 22:1 The Message

Your reputation goes before you. You can only hide for so long. If we are women of character and integrity, we don't have to think twice about our reputations. They are sterling, or admirable. You are worthy of being admired because you have a walk, a reputation fit for a daughter of the king.

Modesty

> "Your beauty should not come from outward adornment, such as braided hair and the wearing of fine clothes. Instead, it should be that of your inner self, the unfading beauty of a gentle and quiet spirit, which is of great worth in God's sight."
>
> 1 Peter 3:3&4

I still struggle from time to time with dressing like a super model of Christ. Especially when we are young, there is so much pressure to dress seductively. And it's fun. Almost every magazine and CD cover has a scantly dressed woman on the front. Guys seem to notice those women a lot more than they do someone fully clothed. It's hard. I totally understand! Jesus never said that it was going to be easy. Remember, we can't walk in the darkness and walk in the light. Don't worry. I'm not going to give you a list of things to wear and things not to. That is not the point. It's all a matter of the heart.

It has been even harder for me since Tony and I have gotten married. All of a sudden I've realized that I can be a sexy woman. I like to dress in soft fabrics and in fitted clothing that show my feminine curves.

That's ok to a degree, but there are many times that I have to ask the Lord to tell me if what I'm wearing glorifies him. I don't always make the right choices, but I am growing just like you. As women of God we need to constantly be in fellowship with the Spirit about how we present the outside of our bodies. We need to ask the Lord if our make-up, hair, and clothes are reflecting the world or if they're reflecting Christ.

Ask yourself the following questions before leaving your house:

#1. Would I be wearing this if Jesus were in the room?
If not, change clothes!

#2. Am I trying to get the attention of a guy?
If yes, change clothes!

#3. Will people even notice my personality or will they be to busy staring at my chest?
If yes, change clothes!

#4. Can I breathe in this outfit?
If not, change clothes!

#5. Are my bra or my underwear showing?
If yes, change clothes!

Carolyn is one of my special sisters in Christ. She is very intelligent but can also be a hilarious goof ball! She has a gorgeous face and frame that could easily be on the cover of a swimsuit magazine. The unique thing about Carolyn, though, is that she chooses not to flaunt the body God gave her. Her reputation is important to her. As a woman of God, she has shared with me that when she goes to her closet she prays, "Jesus what do you want me to wear today? What would you pick out? What would bring you glory?"

Carolyn doesn't hide under a wide piece of sackcloth, but she doesn't wear the uncensored and slutty clothing that many females do. The trends for clothes today are immodest and revealing. A new wave of indecency has engulfed our malls and department stores. We must take a stand. Erika Harold, Miss America 2003, has said, "You must be the change you wish to see in the world." Nothing will change if we don't change!

One of my grandmother's friends has said, "Sheri, the girls these days just don't leave anything for the imagination." Meaning that in her day, men were actually pleasantly surprised on their wedding nights. They hadn't seen the whole package before it was ready to be opened. We need that old tradition to come back in style!

Start today by going through your clothing and throwing out everything you know you shouldn't put on your royal body. Don't think about it; just throw it! Let's start to dazzle the world with God's version of beauty.

Flee

Mandy was a spunky and lively teenage girl who was up on all the latest fashion trends. She even kept a twenty-hour-a-week job just to support her shopping habit. Mandy could barely go two days without heading into the mall to buy the latest sandals, jeans, or pair of earrings. She was like a smoker who couldn't put down her pack of cigarettes for anything. She had accepted Christ as her Savior at youth group several years earlier, but there was still something missing, something she hadn't surrendered. She hadn't even realized that whenever she was sad she would go shopping. Whenever she was lonely she would go shopping. Whenever she was happy with how she did on a social studies exam she would go shopping. Mandy always looked great and she was the authority on trend setting in her Southern Alabama High School.

On a cool spring night God had an appointment with Mandy. Around 9:00PM, she was walking out of the mall after closing. As usual she had one GAP shopping bag dangling at her right side. She walked around the corner toward her car and noticed a small girl sitting on the curb. Mandy was walking quickly, but the Holy Spirit began to tap her on the shoulder. She felt that shiver run down her back and that ache in her stomach.

"Are you all right?" She turned and asked the little girl.

"Yeah, I am just waiting for my mom to pick me up from work," the girl said softly. "Do you work in this mall?"

"Yes. Yes, I do." Mandy said, still wondering why she was even talking to the wide-eyed girl. They spoke for a few more moments. Mandy could sense that this precious girl felt lonely and neglected by her two parents, both of whom were executives in large corporations. Sure, the girl had one bag from Old Navy and another from Macy's, but what she really wanted was love.

Her mother, professionally dressed in a dark, pleated business suit, drove a shiny BMW up to the curb. She motioned for the girl to get in the car. Mandy was just saying "good-bye" as the car quickly drove away.

Mandy threw her bag and purse in the back seat of her car, and just sat in the dark parking lot for a while. The Holy Spirit started to soften her heart and led her to pray for that lonely girl she had just spoken with. As she was praying the Holy Spirit lovingly showed her how she was trying to fill a void in her life with shopping. She was reminded that the money itself and the shopping itself were not sin. The sin was that they were taking the place of God in her life. Money is not a sin, loving money is. Clothes are not a sin, loving clothes is. Cars are not a sin, loving cars is. Marble statues are not sin, loving them is. *"Dear children, keep yourselves from idols." 1 John 5:21*

Mandy began to recognize that she saw her credit cards more often than she saw her Bible. She definitely didn't have much time to see the lost and hurting through her designer sunglasses. She thought about how her room was filled with fashion magazines. She couldn't even remember where she had laid her prayer journal that she had barely started a year ago. In a fresh and soft way God began to show her that she was walking in her flesh and gratifying her desires with the newest pair of Express shorts and Mossimo jackets. Not by his love, grace, and mercy.

That night in her car Mandy asked for forgiveness. She asked the Lord to break the stronghold of shopping in her heart. She wanted to change. It took time and many hours in prayer and Bible study, but she began to notice a difference in her life. She still enjoyed shopping and looking nice, but it wasn't an all-consuming habit anymore. It didn't control her. She had overcome her addiction.

Mandy continued to work in the mall but her paycheck was now spent on giving to others and saving for college. She spent only a small amount on her wardrobe and she looked forward each week to tithing ten percent or more of her income to the Lord's work. During her times of loneliness she began to run into her Father's arms instead of running to Payless Shoes. The coolest thing was that her focus was no longer just on herself and how she looked on the outside. She was much more concerned with what was going on in her heart as well as in the lives of others. At her job she looked for ways to be an encouragement and a blessing to those around her instead of thinking about what outfit she was going to put on for school the next morning. Her transformation is a great example of a young woman who got her priorities in line with Christ. Mandy now loves how she feels inside as she walks in fellowship with her Savior. She did run into that lonely little girl again. This time she had something of value to give her: time. Mandy walked with the girl down to the food court for ice cream. She shared the love and life of Jesus with someone who so desperately needed to be touched by his love.

The Bible says that if we are walking in the Spirit we won't desire to gratify our sinful flesh. It also says to FLEE from those desires. As you and I walk in the Spirit, we hear his voice leading and guiding us. Jesus called him the Counselor. As believers we don't have to guess what the next step is, we can know for sure! We don't have to walk around this planet without a purpose, feeling empty and confused. The Holy Spirit will lead and guide us into all truth as we learn to walk in step with his plan for our lives.

> "But when he, the Spirit of truth, comes, he will guide you into all truth. He will not speak on his own; he will speak only what he hears, and he will tell you what is yet to come. He will bring glory to me by taking from what is mine and make it known to you."
>
> John 16:13&14

To walk in the Spirit is to serve others. I previously shared with you the old woman in Hungary that showed me a true servant's heart. Touched by her example I decided to volunteer at a nursing home during my junior and senior years of high school. Tracy, one of my girlfriends, and I got permission from our school principal to go over to the Good Samaritan Nursing Home on Tuesday and Thursday afternoons. Tracy and I would read to the residents, help them get down to the dining hall for meals, play games, and do puzzles. I was touched to hear several of the residents talk about their lives. Many of the men and women eagerly shared with us lessons that they had learned and special memories from their pasts. One tiny white-haired woman would show me pictures of her children, her grandchildren, and her great-grandchildren almost every time I visited her room. It was funny how she would forget that she had shown them to me over a dozen times before. Another older gentleman shared remarkable stories about his youth, growing up during the Great Depression.

Some people would call what Tracy and I did community service. I call it walking right!

Have you considered volunteering at a nursing home? What about spending a few hours a week mentoring and being a friend to a young girl from your city? How about cleaning a senior citizen's home once a week and not asking for anything in return? Have you ever wondered what it would be like to spend time reading to cancer patients or singing to babies with HIV? Why don't you start a morning prayer group or Bible study in your school? Why don't you start a mail drive to send encouraging letters to our soldiers stationed in the Middle East, Afghanistan, or Korea? There are so many ways that we can reach out to serve those hurting and in need. You have a special gift, sister, that someone is waiting to receive. Only you can give it away!

Let's learn a lesson from the acorn. The acorn is a little thing but it produces a large oak tree that in turn produces fruit, is a home for birds, helps keep our atmosphere clean, and is shade for us on a hot summer day! We may be small, but we have a big DADDY!

The starfish thrower

My dad told me a story about a young man walking along a sandy beach. It was growing dark when he noticed a shadow off in the distance. He approached slowly and watched as an older gentleman picked up starfish and threw them back into the ocean. The young man stood back a while, working up the courage to ask the man what he was doing. Finally he opened his mouth. "Sir, may I ask what you are doing with those starfish?"

The older man smiled, "I am rescuing these starfish. I must throw them back into the surf before they die."

The young man nodded. He scanned as far as he could see along the shoreline. There were so many starfish, more than he could ever hope to count. Hesitantly he asked, "But sir, there are so many starfish on this beach. Many will die. You can't save them all. How do you think you can make a difference?"

Once again the older man smiled. Bending down, he picked up another starfish and tossed it into the ocean. He said, "For that one starfish, I made a difference."

Talk Right

You are probably thinking, "Ok, Sheri. I know that models need to eat right and walk right, but they don't need to speak to do their job." You are basically right in this regard. Models don't need to talk much during their stroll down the runway. However, they need to speak well during interviews. And commercial models or pageant contestants need to talk to be successful in their fields. In fact, talking is the most important part of their job. When I was Miss Iowa, I didn't spend much of my time riding in parades and or simply walking around looking pretty. The majority of my time was spent *talking* with youth, adults, teachers, parents, government officials, community leaders, and civic organizations. It was imperative that my speeches were successful! I had to learn to talk right. No "um," "uh," "yah," or "but."

Talking right is important in our quest to be super models of Christ. My mom told me when I was a young girl that *God spoke the universe into existence*. All it took was a spoken word to bring the galaxies in line, to set the stars shining and to start the earth rotating around the sun. We recognize the familiar words in Genesis when God said, "Let there be light." And there was light.

Solomon, the wisest man who ever lived, had a lot to say about the words that come out of our mouths:

> *"An anxious heart weighs a man down, but a kind word cheers him up."*
> PROVERBS 12:25

> *"A gentle answer turns away wrath, but a harsh word stirs up anger."*
> PROVERBS 15:1

> *"A word aptly spoken is like apples of gold in settings of silver."*
> PROVERBS 25:11

It's amazing how just one or two words can change an entire situation. Just like when Jesus rebuked the wind and waves by saying "Be still!" or when a bride and groom on their wedding day say the words "I do" and their lives are forever changed.

James also tells us that life and death are in the tongue. "*When we put bits into the mouths of horses to make them obey us, we can turn the whole animal. Or take ships as an example. Although they are so large and are driven by strong winds, they are steered by a very small rudder wherever the pilot wants to go. Like-*

wise, the tongue is a small part of the body, but it makes great boasts. Consider what a great forest is set on fire by a small spark. The tongue also is a fire, a world of evil among the parts of the body. It corrupts the whole person, sets the whole course of his life on fire, and is itself set on fire by hell." (James 3:3-6) Those are pretty powerful words. When was the last time your tongue got you into that much trouble? Could it be yesterday when you yelled those piercing words at your mom as you slammed your bedroom door? Could it have been last week as you cut a friend down during cheerleading practice because she didn't jump high enough in your last routine? Could it have been last month when you told your brother you hated him because he refused to let you have your way? Could it have been a few days ago when you cussed at your teacher under your breath because he gave you to much homework? Could it have been over a year ago when you and some of your closest friends were gossiping about the new girl and the reputation that followed her from her previous school?

God clearly tells us in Ephesians 4:28 not to let any unwholesome talk come out of our mouths, but only words that build others up. I love how *The Message* phrases it,

> *"Watch the way you talk. Let nothing foul or dirty come out of your mouth. Say only what helps, each word a gift. Don't grieve God. Don't break his heart. His Holy Spirit, moving and breathing in you, is the most intimate part of your life, making you fit for himself. Don't take such a gift for granted. Make a clean break with all cutting, backbiting, pro-*

> *fane talk. Be gentle with one another, sensitive. Forgive one another as quickly and thoroughly as God in Christ forgave you."*

I was standing in my school lunch line waiting for my chocolate milk and greasy cheeseburger when I heard someone in the back of the line laughing about the shoes I was wearing. It wasn't so much what she said but how she said it. I didn't go to the back of the line and confront her. I was too embarrassed. It hurt to know that I recognized the voice speaking those words. She was one of my so-called friends, a girl I had played with on our high school basketball team for three years. Have you had a situation like that happen to you? Have you heard all the girls on the back of the bus gossiping about you, how you look, or they way you played during the game that night? It hurts, doesn't it?

In junior high I had a habit of tossing my long brown hair around. If it was sitting on my shoulders I would play with it and gently toss it behind my head. I really hadn't noticed that it had become a habit until I heard the guys sitting behind me in choir laughing about me and mimicking me with their hands. I turned back to look at them as they continued to laugh and mock me. I slowly sunk down in my seat and fought back the tears. It didn't even matter that I barely knew those guys; it just hurt to be made fun of. Whoever said "sticks and stones may break my bones, but words will never hurt me" was wrong!

It's hard to understand how we can continue to talk badly about other people even when we know how much it hurts to be on the receiving end. Jesus knows how we feel. He was mocked and made fun of. He knows how it feels to have warm tears run down our cheeks when we feel betrayed by the words of a close friend. He was betrayed too.

Watching Judas kiss Jesus' cheek in Mel Gibson's movie *The Passion of The Christ*, was a staunch reminder that Jesus understands how betrayal hurts. He understands everything we go through, sis.

> "For we do not have a high priest who is unable to sympathies with our weaknesses, but we have one who has been tempted in every way, as we are – yet was without sin. Let us then approach the throne of grace with confidence, so that we may receive mercy and find grace to help us in our time of need."
>
> *Hebrews 4:15&16*

Our job as super models is to use the words that come out of our mouths to build others up, not tear them down. Our job is to encourage with our speech, not hinder and bruise with our words. Paul, Timothy, and Silas wrote to the Thessalonian church,

> "Therefore encourage each other and build each other up..."
>
> *1 Thessalonians 5:11*

All it takes is for one brave girl to stand up in the midst of a crowd of gossipers and say, "This isn't right. I'm outta here until ya'll find something good to talk about." Sometimes all it takes is for us to walk away from the crowd and the others will feel conviction just by us leaving. A wise man once said, "Preach Christ every day and if necessary, use words." Just by your simple action of not putting up with gossip, belittling, and slandering other people, you will make a major difference in this world.

A sad fact is that getting a group of woman together to talk has a tendency to bring out the worst in us. In Proverbs 10 it says that a chattering fool comes to ruin. Later in Proverbs 20:19 it says, "*A gossip betrays a confidence, so avoid a man who talks too much.*" The Lord tells us over and over again to be careful about what comes out of our mouths. The more words we speak without thinking, the more sins we need to ask for forgiveness from. I am preaching to myself here.

Super models keep a tight rein on their tongues. We don't just blurt out the first thing that comes to our minds. We think about what we say before we say it. As my Grandma Jean says, "If you don't have anything good to say, don't say anything at all."

You are what you say you are

Darlene and I became instant friends. She has a contagious laugh and kind heart. Her fantastic personality makes me crave spending time with her! She has a great sense of humor and is always looking for ways to build you up with her words. Darlene has beautiful dark eyes, hair, and skin. Her father is from Saudi Arabia and her mother is from the United States. She looked to me like an Egyptian Queen. She is very tall and has a bit of a stocky build. She is truly gorgeous! She confided in me one night over a box of mini-donuts that for most of her life she wished that she looked different. She felt overweight and ugly. She wanted to have white skin, believing that would prevent her from being discriminated against. She longed to be a little shorter so more guys would ask her out. Darlene hated feeling like she was always the friend, never the girlfriend. Over and over she told me things that she wanted to change about herself. It was like she saw a completely different person when she looked in the mirror than I saw standing in front of me. She had put herself down so often that she was stuck thinking of herself like that. I guess when you hear something long enough, you begin to believe it's true.

Another girl I know has a life that many would envy, but is constantly complaining. She complains about her body, how much money she doesn't have, her car, and her parents. Negativity flows out of her mouth in a steady stream. I don't think she even realizes it.

If you look in the mirror every morning and say out loud or think deep down inside, "I am so ugly. I'm a pathetic waste of oxygen. I hate my nose that sticks out so far! I can't stand my round hips and those freckles have to go!" Do you know that you have just become who you say you are?

My pastor made it known to our congregation that 90% of what Americans think is negative? That probably means that almost 90% of what they say is negative too, especially to themselves. Why don't we as super models start a new trend to bring that statistic down? I'm not talking about being fake or using positive thinking just for the sake of doing it. I mean to honestly make an effort to speak the things that the Lord told us to speak about. Things glorifying to him, that lift up instead of tear down.

God must look down at his creation and cry when he sees us talking to ourselves like that. Again, "*Finally, brothers, whatever is true, whatever is noble, whatever is right, whatever is pure, whatever is lovely, whatever is admirable - if anything is excellent or praiseworthy - think about such things.*" *Philippians 4:8.* Our speech and our thinking are basically one and the same. If we are thinking the way God wants us to think, we will talk the way God wants us to talk. He wants *good* words to come out of our mouths. He wants our tongues to be vessels of life, not death.

Joyce Myers wrote a fantastic book called *Me And My Big Mouth!* The title made me laugh when I picked it up off the bookshelf. Joyce reminds us that what we say is what we will get! Have you ever noticed how people who talk about feeling sick all the time *are* always sick? Have you noticed how people who say they are going to fail a test usually fail it? Most of what we say and confess out of our mouths comes true. Cherry Meadows, one of my mentors says, "If you don't want it, don't say it!"

Let's read over Joshua 6:1-20.

> Now Jericho was tightly shut up because of the Israelites. No one went out and no one came in.

Then the Lord said to Joshua, "See, I have delivered Jericho into your hands, along with its king and its fighting men. March around the city once with all the armed men. Do this for six days. Have seven priests carry trumpets of rams' horns in front of the ark. On the seventh day, march around the city seven times, with the priests blowing the trumpets. When you hear them sound a long blast on the trumpets, have all the people give a loud shout; then the wall of the city will collapse and the people will go up, every man straight in."

So Joshua son of Nun called the priests and said to them, "Take up the ark of the covenant of the Lord and have seven priests carry trumpets in front of it." And he ordered the people, "Advance! March around the city, with the armed guard ahead of the ark of the Lord."

When Joshua had spoken to the people, the seven priests carrying the seven trumpets before the Lord went forward, blowing their trumpets and the ark of the Lord's covenant followed them. The armed guard marched ahead of the priests who blew the trumpets, and the rear guard followed the ark. All this time the trumpets were sounding. But Joshua had commanded the people, "Do not give a war cry, do not raise your voices, do not say a word until the day I tell you to shout. Then shout!" So he had the ark of the Lord carried around the city, circling it once. Then the people returned to the camp and spent the night there.

Joshua got up early the next morning and the priests took up the ark of the Lord. The seven priests carrying the seven trumpets went forward, marching before the ark of the Lord and blowing the trumpets. The armed men went ahead of them and the rear guard followed the ark of the Lord, while the trumpets kept sounding. So on the second day they marched around the city once and returned to camp. They did this for six days.

On the seventh day, they got up at daybreak and marched around the city seven times in the same manner, except that on that day they circled the city seven times. The seventh time around, when the priests sounded the trumpet blast, Joshua commanded the people, "Shout! For the Lord has given you the city! The city and all that is in it are to be devoted to the Lord. Only Rahab the prostitute and all who are with her in her house shall be spared, because she hid the spies we sent. But keep away from the devoted things, so that you will not bring about your own destruction by taking ay of them. Otherwise you will make the camp of Israel liable to destruction and bring trouble on it. All the silver and gold and the articles of bronze and iron are sacred to the Lord and must go into his treasury."

When the trumpets sounded, the people shouted, and at the sound of the trumpet, when the people gave a loud shout, the wall collapsed; so every man charged strait in and they took the city.

What an awesome miracle, huh? God showed the Israelites that he was in charge, that they had no need to fear new life in the Promised Land. Their God was bigger than any wall that they would face and he is certainly bigger than any wall you and I might face! Bigger than walls of pride, walls of fear, walls of hurt, and walls of doubt.

Wasn't it totally wild that Joshua told the people not to say a single word until he told them to shout? Why do you think he did that? Can you just imagine what might have happened if he would have let them chatter during those seven days? My idea is that we may have heard conversations like the following: "Joshua is crazy man! How could the wall possibly fall down just by us shouting? Hasn't he looked at the wall? It's huge!" "I'm afraid, what if those people from Jericho decide to attack us first? We all may be dead before the seventh day." "My throat hurts. I don't think I can shout very loud. It will strain my vocal cord too much!" "My feet hurt! We've been marching around this stupid city for almost a week and I'm ready for a break!"

I believe that Joshua trusted the Lord. He knew that God was going to do a great miracle. He certainly didn't want the negative talk of the people to mess up what God had planned. Joshua knew that they could void all that God was doing if he let their mouths run with negative words. Silence for seven days was what it took for them to see a miracle. Do you think you could be quiet for seven days? Better yet, do you think you could go without saying anything negative for seven days? What about just for one day or even one hour? You would be amazed at the miracles that would take place in your life if you accomplished that goal!

I have a mission statement for my life that I read out loud to myself almost every day. It goes like this:

> "I am a strong, spirit-filled, godly woman. My eyes are fixed on Jesus and my thoughts are continuously focused on him. I hunger and thirst for the Word. I meditate on it day and night. I am under construction and My Father loves me completely. My greatest joy comes from knowing him and resting in his presence. My attitude is always, "I will do," and never, "I will try." I am a winner and I'm going to win. I was created and predestined for greatness. I am going to accomplish my dreams and bear fruit in all things. I am going to meet new people every day and look for ways to be a servant and a blessing to everyone. Divine appointments and angels are part of my daily life. I have a zest for life and am full of enthusiasm. I am forgiven! I will fully obey the Lord and follow his commands today! The fruit of my womb is blessed. I am blessed in every way and every place I go, favor is upon me. Everything my hand touches will prosper! My enemies must flee from me because the same power that raised Jesus from the dead lives in me. The Lord has granted me abundant prosperity and I will walk in all his ways. I am healthy, fit, whole, and healed! I am a wife of noble character. I love Tony completely and will honor, cherish, and trust him the rest of my life. Each day is a gift for us to share and I will

forever be his best friend! For charm is deceptive and beauty is fleeting; but a woman who fears the Lord is to be praised. I am a woman of prayer. I am the best wife, mother, daughter, granddaughter, and friend. I love people. Today, everything my hand finds to do, I will do it with all my might because I am fearfully and wonderfully made!"

When I speak those commanding words of life over myself, I feel energized! I feel refreshed! I simply applied verses from the Word of God, confessing them over my life. When I speak to myself that way, there is no room for Satan to weasel his way into my thought life. Unlike my favorite Swiss cheese, there are no holes in my spirit. When you and I speak the Word of God over our lives he will manifest his purpose in our hearts. When we pray like Jesus did, "Let *your* will be done Father," we leave room for God to do what he wants on your behalf. He is just waiting to bless us, sister. It's time for you to make a mission statement!

In her book *Living The Abundant Life* Paula White says, "God will never give you a vision without giving you provision. Everything God told you to do, He not only will qualify you to do, but He will equip you to do. God's people are supposed to live in abundance and overflow!"

Let's throw negative thinking and speaking out the door of our lives! There is no room for a super model to let Satan deceive her with those vices. Or should I say there is no room for "stinkin-thinkin!"

There is a powerful book written by Bruce Wilkenson called, *The Prayer of Jabez*. Bruce's wife Darlene wrote a book specifically for us girls called, *The Prayer of Jabez for Women.* Jabez's actual prayer is recorded in 1 Chronicles 4:9 and10,

> *"Now Jabez was more honorable than his brothers, and his mother called his name Jabez, saying, 'Because I bore him in pain.' And Jabez called on the Lord of Israel saying, 'Oh that You would bless me indeed, and enlarge my territory, that your hand would be with me, and that You would keep me from evil, that I may not cause pain!' So God granted him what he requested."*

I love what Darlene says on the last page of her book.

> Since we near the end of this book, let's talk about the end of the story. Do you remember how it ended? "So God granted him what he requested." (1 Chronicles 4:10)
>
> Let me ask you something. If someone were telling your story at the end of your life, how would it read? Would it describe you as more honorable? Would it talk about how you prayed? How would it describe your lifestyle?
>
> If you sincerely pray the prayer of Jabez on a regular basis and respond to God's hand in your life, there's one thing you can know for sure - and that's the *end* of your story. I have no doubt that it will read, "So God granted her what she requested."

> But the end isn't here yet, is it? There's still so much to do, learn, and see. Life with God is an endlessly exciting adventure. And God doesn't want you to miss one moment of it. That's why He wants to hear your voice today, asking Him for His blessings and for a bigger view of all that's possible. It's time to enjoy the parade!

That endless adventure is determined by what comes out of our mouths. Just like Jabez requested of the Lord what he wanted for his life, we need to do the same. We need to speak the truth of what God has for our lives and not the lies this world subscribes to.

When I was eight years old, my parents came up with an idea to help our family think before we spoke. They called it "The Negative Jar." Ah, the dreaded clear glass negative jar! Every time my dad, my mom, my brother, or myself would say something negative, we had to put a quarter in the jar. A quarter may not seem like much, but they add up fast. If we yelled unkind words to each other, in dropped a quarter. If we said, "I can't," in went a quarter. That trivial jar began to fill up before we knew it.

When the jar started to overflow all four of us began to pay much better attention to that little hole between our teeth. We learned that we had to keep control over our tongues. It turned out to be a family project that we learned an immense truth from. We used the money from the negative jar to pay for part of a vacation to a water park the following summer. Yes, everything works out for good.

Lastly, talking right includes telling the truth. Satan is the father of lies as well as the great deceiver.

> "He was a murderer from the beginning, not holding to the truth, for there is no truth in him. When he lies, he speaks his native language, for he is a liar, and the father of lies."
>
> *John 4:44b and 45*

Telling the truth at all times is very hard. Lying is tempting when we want to get out of a test, talk to certain people, or are nervous about being punished for something. Lying feels like an easy and painless way out at the moment. It leads to even greater pain, though. The Bible says that the truth shall set us free. That means that if we lie we are in bondage or slavery. We will never be free unless we speak the truth. Are you a person that people can trust? How's your reputation in the honesty department? Do you keep your word when you tell someone you are going to do something for them?

Let's make this our prayer: "Father, thank you for giving me this mouth. Lord, I want my voice to be a vessel for you to work through. I don't want lies, filth, swearing, or gossip to come from my lips. I am a new creation and I want to live this great adventure for you! Thank you for cleaning and purifying my mouth and my thoughts, making them obedient to you. I am going to be a super model that is talking right. Thank you for granting my request, Daddy. In Jesus name, amen!"

A Love Worth Waiting For

As I sat down to write a name for this chapter, I just couldn't decide. Should it be sexual purity? How far is *too* far? Sex? Finding the man of your dreams? Should I even date for that matter? I guess it could be all five of them. Before you read on, ask the Holy Spirit to open your heart to hear what He is trying to tell you. Each one of us is unique and is at a different place in our walk with the Lord. You may say, "Sheri, I don't need to read anything on sexual abstinence because I've already had sex. It's over for me. I've blown it." You may be someone else who says, "This is great! I needed some encouragement today on purity!" You might also be saying, "Not again, I have been hearing this message from my parents, my youth pastor, my older sister, and my Aunt Edith. I've had enough. Thanks but no thanks, Sheri." No matter where you are right now or how you're feeling, I suggest you read on.

Yesterday I wasn't feeling very well. My stomach was going through one of those churning moments and I had a terrible headache. I plopped down on my couch, threw a worn blanket on top of me, and turned on the TV. I don't recall the names of the two sitcoms I watched, but they had one thing very much in common. They both showed a terribly ungodly view of sex. I guess it's just normal today. No big deal. You can't turn on the television or pop in a DVD without seeing the world's version of love: LUST!

Bill O'Reilly, the popular host of *The O'Reilly Factor* on the Fox News channel, wrote this in his July 9, 2001, online article: "One of the biggest problems we have in this country is one rarely discussed in civilized society: the sexualization of America's children has reached a crisis point, and the kids are getting hurt." He goes on to write, "Today, even little children are exposed to sex on an almost daily basis. Sex ed often starts early in public schools. MTV is one big sex extravaganza, and many of TV's most popular programs, like 'Friends,' are full of sexual situations and innuendos. The Boy Scouts are under fire for not accepting 'avowed' homosexual scoutmasters. And even clothing catalogs aimed at the young border on soft porn. Don't be surprised if HBO creates a series called 'Sex and the Kiddie'."

I agree with what Mr. O'Reilly wrote, and I am disgusted with our world's evil view of what God meant to be 100% pure. I simply can't understand how meeting someone one afternoon at a party and jumping in bed with them that night is very exciting. How can you trust your body to someone you don't even know?

On the other hand, I do understand how marvelous it is to be married to a man with whom you feel totally secure and safe. I know that it's holy when those fireworks go off in a Christian married couple's bedroom! We don't have to be afraid of anything. There is no shame, no confusion, and no lust. Just pure intoxicating love! There is peace, joy, happiness, and even laughter! True romance!

You don't have to worry about awkwardly getting out of bed and leaving to go to separate homes. The Christian couple is home. They can fall asleep relaxed in each other's loving hands. There is no shame or guilt. There is no wondering if pain or sickness will come out of the mistake of having sex outside of wedlock.

Life or Death

God made sex. Having sex is a covenant with God, you, and your mate. He made it a wonderful and holy experience. An entire book of the Bible shows a godly relationship, godly passions, godly purity, and a fantastic sex life! Song of Solomon shows sacrifice and commitment, a holy courtship, and a marriage made in heaven. Solomon reminds us not to awaken love until the right time. That right time is in a Christian marriage. Not before. *"Do not arouse or awaken love until it so desires." Song of Songs 2:9*

This is a subject that I feel an intense burden to share with you. Look around you. Your friends and mine are dying because we don't have the self-control to abstain until marriage. It's a deadly disease that has infiltrated our schools and, even worse, our own church youth groups. Life and death are hanging in the balance.

I am earnestly praying, for you sister. I am praying that one of your highest goals and biggest dreams in life would be purity. Put a poster up in your room that screams out purity every morning when you get out of bed. Make a banner on your bedroom door! Write the word "purity" on your hand so you can see it all day long. Talk to your friends, neighbors, and even strangers about the awesome gift of purity!

> *"Love the Lord you God with all your heart and with all your soul and with all your strength. These commandments that I give you today are to be upon your hearts. Impress them on your children. Talk about them when you sit at home and when you walk along the road, when you lie down and when you getup. Tie them as symbols on your hands and bind them on your foreheads. Write them on the doorframes of you houses and on your gates."*
>
> DEUTERONOMY *6:5-8*

Run

> "Flee sexual immorality. All other sins a man commits are outside his body, but he who sins sexually sins against his own body. Do you not know that your body is a temple of the Holy Spirit, who is in you,

> whom you received from God? You are not your own; you were bought at a price. Therefore honor God with your body."
>
> 1 Corinthians 6:18-20

It's as simple as that! God says to FLEE sexual sins. RUN AWAY FROM THEM!! It should be black and white. Are you married? Great, then have sex with your spouse. Are you not married? DON'T have sex! It couldn't get more basic than that.

Pam Stenzel is one of the greatest speakers I have ever heard on this topic. I've listened to her tapes over and over again. She reminds us that every day in America there are 12,000 teenagers that contract a sexually transmitted disease. 12,000! That means there are at least 12,000 teenagers a day having intercourse or oral sex. Yes, oral sex IS sex. No matter if former President Clinton thinks so or not. Sin is sin.

Pam also shares that there are over 30 different kinds of sexually transmitted diseases. You don't have to get AIDS to die. Other STD's kill too. And did you know that a pregnant teen girl in America carries on average 2.3 sexually transmitted diseases? It's sick and sad. It's heartbreaking. All those girls have one of three painful choices to make. #1. Have the baby and raise the baby. #2 Have the baby and give it up for adoption. #3. Kill the baby through abortion. All three of those choices are painful and will be hard to live with, my dear.

> "Do you not know that the wicked will not inherit the kingdom of God? Do not be deceived: Neither the sexually immoral nor

> idolaters not adulterers, not male prostitutes nor homosexual offenders will inherit the kingdom of God."
>
> 1 Corinthians 6:9 and 10

God didn't tell us to wait to have sex until marriage to punish us. He told us to wait to protect us. A goldfish is safe and secure in the clear water of his fish bowl. If he chooses to jump out of his fish bowl to explore beyond the boundaries set for him, he will die. Fish can't live outside water and you and I can't truly live without the boundaries the Lord set in place for us. I pray that Jesus would become so real to you that you couldn't imagine letting him down. You couldn't imagine jumping out of the fishbowl. You couldn't imagine living without his protective boundaries.

Alexa's story

Alexa was a sweet girl I met some time ago. She was an A student and a leader on her school track team. She attended a private school and even went to Bible class every morning. Alexa went to several retreat weekends like Impact, Acquire The Fire, and True Love Waits. At each of those events she made a deeper commitment to wait to have sex until marriage. She even made a strong commitment that she wouldn't go past light kissing in her physical relationships with guys. She wrote her commitment down on a piece of paper in her Bible and began praying for her future mate. Several of her friends did the same thing.

The summer before Alexa's junior year in high school, she was at a summer camp teaching Bible school to elementary age kids. It was great seeing them come to understand salvation better! There was never a dull moment and laughter filled the campsite. There were 14 other teens that were helping with the camp that year. They all met together every morning to pray for the children they were teaching. On the weekends they would hang out together before the next group of kids arrived. Over time Alexa developed a deep friendship with a guy named Brett. Brett had blue eyes, sandy blond hair, and smelled like fresh pine. These things attracted Alexa to him, but most of all she was attracted to his love for Christ. He was one of those guys who led the prayer groups and Bible studies. He was kind, thoughtful, and always had something encouraging to say to other members of the camp staff. By the end of the summer Brett and Alexa were dating. All the other teens thought they made the perfect couple. As the summer camp ended they all promised to keep in touch. It was going to be pretty easy for Brett and Alexa because they lived just 20 minutes away from each other in two small towns in Minnesota.

The phone calls came almost every day, their emails and instant messages were frequent, and they saw each other almost every weekend. When Brett's homecoming approached, they made plans for what they would wear and what kind of flowers looked good with Alexa's dress. The love between them was growing and they had a deep bond of friendship. Alexa loved dreaming about her and Brett's future. She believed they would get married one day. For now though, it was almost like they were married. They spent holidays with each other's families, exchanged gifts, and were pretty much inseparable. Their parents were happy too. Who wouldn't want their son or daughter to be dating such a wonderful young Christian?

One humid summer night Brett and Alexa sat beside a lake and talked for several hours. They talked about last year at summer camp and how they were both so thankful that God had given them each other. Up until this point they had only kissed a few times, but the struggle not to go farther was getting harder. They were so close emotionally and yet so far apart physically. It just didn't fit. As the stars twinkled and moonlight shone over the lake, Brett reached out for Alexa's soft face. He looked into her eyes and gently told her how much he loved her and wanted to be with her forever. It felt right. They kissed and drew closer on the grassy shore. Alexa felt her body press against his as tingles ran up and down her spine. The kissing got stronger and pretty soon they were laying on the ground wrapped in each other's starving arms. Both of them kept feeling like they should shout out "No, stop!" But they longed for each other. The will and self-control they thought they had seemed to vanish into thin air. The time passed quickly and they knew they needed to get back to Brett's parent's house for a family barbeque. Alexa, hurried and ashamed, put her clothes back on and Brett walked to his car. They did not speak; the drive seemed to last for hours.

The next day neither one called the other. They didn't know what to say. Yes, they loved each other. Yes, it felt good to have sex. Brett felt stronger and more like a man, and yet at the same time he felt ugly and selfish. He felt like he had not only betrayed his sweet girlfriend, but more importantly his Savior. Alexa lay on her bed crying for hours that night. She felt dirty and very unloved. She had felt so protected by Brett at first, and now all she felt was alone, abandoned. Could she be pregnant? Would her parents find out? Would things ever be the same? Could God still love her and have a plan for her life? Was it all her fault? Why didn't her boundaries work? They always had in the past.

How do you think the story ends? Only by God's forgiveness and grace did they both overcome their pasts. Alexa and Brett couldn't face the temptation any more and decided to break up a few weeks later. Darkness and pain shadowed the closeness they had once felt. They would have to live with their mistake, ask for forgiveness from their future spouses, and try to forget that night by the lake.

Most stories like that don't have happy endings. Sure, there is forgiveness because of Jesus' death on the cross, but how much more wonderful would it have been if Alexa and Brett had stuck to the decision they had both made to remain sexually pure until marriage? It would have been an amazing testimony to the world of God's *true* and *patient* love. A love worth waiting for.

Cindy's story

Cindy began having sex at 9 years old. Her parents were divorced and she had a much older sister who invited guys over to their house all the time. These guys saw young Cindy as nothing more than a piece of meat. Cindy felt unloved and lonely. She had a very low self-esteem. She hid behind food, and became overweight. She barely even knew her biological dad.

Cindy told me that she remembers trying to block out the pain, trying to rationalize that all these guys truly cared for her in some way. Her body really wasn't her own and she didn't like herself very much. She didn't feel worthy of love. By the time she reached her teen years she couldn't even remember how many guys she had been with. Even after she came to know Christ when a friend invited her to his youth group, the sexual sin continued. She had a longing for it. She thought that was the only way to get close to someone and to feel special. She reminded me that all she really wanted was love.

I can't tell you how Cindy's story ends. I pray for her and ask God to heal the brokenness she feels. It's her choice, though. She can either *flee* or stay right where she is in pain and unrest.

You might have a similar story to Alexa or Cindy, afraid that you might never be pure again. I have good news for you, sister. You can be! You can ask the Lord to cleanse you of that sin and make you new, a virgin all over again. Rebecca St. James calls it "being a recycled virgin!" God can and will make you new again. Guaranteed.

One of my friends, Danielle, showed me a great analogy. If I handed you a new green $50 dollar bill, would you take it? Sure you would. Who wouldn't except a gift like that? What if I had folded the bill in half twice? Would you still take it? Sure you would. It's still good. What if I crumpled it up into a ball?

Would you accept it them? Again, you would. Lastly, what if I dropped it in the dirt and stepped on it? You would still take it. You would just dust it off and clean it up because it still has value now matter what is done to it! $50 dollars is $50 dollars. The value doesn't change because the bill has been crumpled. In the same way, you are still worth your full value no matter what you have been through. The price tag that God put on you at birth hasn't changed. It is still priceless!

I am privileged to know many young super models that have waited or are still waiting for their husbands. They are saving that special gift for just one exclusive man. I'm one of those ladies. When I first started writing this book five years ago I was a virgin waiting for my mate. Now, I am a married woman who is so very thankful that I did wait. The best gift I have ever given my husband was my purity.

I want to apologize to you for all those adults that have said, "It's OK. Everyone is doing it." "Your hormones are going crazy, girl, and you can't control them." "It's much too hard to expect abstinence." "You'll fail." "Just use a condom and some birth control."

People who make those statements make me beyond angry! I become furious when I hear adults that should be protecting you helping you make that fatal mistake. Guidance counselors hand out condoms in your schools. The pastors of churches who agree with those guidance counselors. People who work for Planned Parenthood or maybe even your own parents expect so little from you. They believe you won't have the self-control to wait. I feel sorry for those people. They are completely blinded by Satan's lies.

I beg you to listen to people like Joshua Harris, who wrote *I Kissed Dating Good-bye*. I want you to hear from solid mentors like Elizabeth Elliot, Pam Stenzel, Ron Luce, Joy Williams, Rebecca St. James, Tara Dawn Christensen (Miss America 1997), Steven Curtis Chapman, Susie Shellenberger, and Dannah Gresh.

I wish you could hear the stories of all my friends, all the young women I have been privileged to meet who have waited or are waiting for their mates! Gals like my close friend Mona who married her godly man Chris a week after Tony and I wed. I want you to hear true stories like Tracy's and Courtney's, who dated their husbands for over four years and yet through perseverance, remained virgins while dating. I would love for you to sit down with Brooke and her new husband Rick to hear how they got engaged in Thailand on a mission trip. It would be so exciting for you to hear the story of Carolyn Goad who waited until her 30's before God brought her the man of her dreams. She calls him "her miracle." She waited patiently for God all those years and even fasted for 40 days when the Lord told her to in regards to her future mate. I wish you could sit down on a rocking chair with my Grandma Ethel and hear her story about getting pregnant on her wedding night and the entire small town in South Dakota gossiping that she just couldn't have been a virgin when she and Robert got married. But she was! I want you to know that there is a girl named Szilvi from Budapest, Hungary, who came to know the Lord several years ago and began a new waiting for a godly husband. God brought her Peter. The Lord honored her obedience to him when she became a new creation in Christ! I have many other friends who are rejoicing in godly marriages now because they waited for their husbands. Friends like Sarah, Amber, Rebecca, Shakilia, and Megan. I also want you to know that there are others like you who are patiently waiting this very hour! You are not alone. There are thousands of young women, like you, who have made a bold stand for abstinence and purity in their schools, youth groups, at their jobs, and in their communities.

And it's not just us girls who are waiting. It's guys too! There are so many guys I personally know who are men of integrity, who would never compromise their faith or yours for momentary pleasures. They are virgins who are waiting for that pure girl God is preparing for them. Young men I know like Will, Greg, Michael, Luke, Scott, Adam, and John.

For those of you who are virgins, I pray that you will be a virgin not just in your skin, but also in your heart. Virginity is something sacred, something so pure that you almost have to whisper it. It's something to shelter, to protect, and to cherish. It's something to be proud of! You are in a group that is superior in quality! You are in a club that is filled with members whose hearts are pure gold because they have been tested by fire. You are a rare stone, my sister. A gem!

The waiting game

You might be saying, "I'm waiting, Sheri, but it gets harder every day. What are some practical things I can do to help me wait?"

I have received a lot of ideas from different gals I've talked with. Sarah said, "I pray for my boyfriend every night before I go to sleep. He prays for me too. As we pray for each other it reminds us how we respect one another. By praying we are also reminded how precious our virginity is to both of us."

Stephanie told me, "My boyfriend and I spend the majority of our time together in group activities. Not so much movie renting and snuggling on the couch, but more roller blading and going out for pizza with friends. "

Reagan said, "It helps my boyfriend and me to go out to movies at theaters where there are a lot of people around. It keeps temptations away when we meet for fun activities with our youth group and praise band."

Hannah told me, "Since my boyfriend and I spend a great deal of time with each other's families, they help to keep us accountable. We spend time getting to know each other during family outings, meal times, and boating on the lake near my home with my siblings and parents."

Finally Marisa said, "I choose not to date all together. I am waiting until I am finished with school and could actually get married. I mean, what's the point of dating for no reason? I have guy friends, but that's all they are, friends. I have made a commitment to wait for the man of my dreams while not breaking anyone's heart in the process. Why would I want to break the heart of one of my brothers in Christ? I know choosing not to date is a radical idea, but it's the best one for sure! More young women should choose this path.

It's freeing! I am using this time while I'm single to focus on God. I have the freedom to go, do, and be all he wants for me while I'm young!"

I agree with Marisa, knowing that you can wait! I believe in you and I know that there is more to you than others think is possible. I know that you're a leader and you're waiting with a purpose. That purpose may even be singleness. You're thinking "Oh! No! Singleness forever?" Well, it's possible that God has plans for you that are far greater than getting married. Purity is so much more than sexuality in marriage. It's a life that is open and holy before God. In the New Testament Paul had something to say about singleness.

> "Now for the matters you wrote about: It is good for a man not to marry. But since there is so much immorality, each man should have his own wife, and each woman her own husband. The husband should fulfill his marital duty to his wife, and likewise the wife to her husband."
>
> 1 Corinthians 7:1-3

When we are single we can be completely focused on the things of God. A married woman must also think about her household. We must care for our husband and our children. We spend hours cleaning, cooking, and for some women, holding a job outside the home too. I consider it an honor to be a wife and mother. It is my highest calling! It's an amazing and wonderful gift! However, when I was single I spent a lot more time devoted to ministry in the church and volunteer work. Now my main ministry focus is my home. And for the most part, I had more time for devotions, Bible study, and prayer before I had a family. Now those things are still priorities, but I don't have as much *time*. Therefore, sis, remember that singleness is a blessing and should be looked at that way. Enjoy being single! Focus on what God has for you while you're single.

Your wedding night

Most of us dream of having that fairytale wedding some day and spending our life with the man of our dreams. That's a great dream to have. A more important one, though, should be the purity leading up to that dream. Our goal should be to reach that important night in our life without regrets, without having to look back into our past of haunting memories and hurting hearts.

So many girls have asked me, "Sheri, how far can I go with a guy before it becomes sin?" That is a hard question. Why don't you ask your dad, mom, or youth pastor? They would likely give you the same answer that I am going to, or maybe even a better answer.

I believe it's all in our motives. If we hold hands with a guy, sooner or later it leads to him putting his arm around us. We feel special then and that usually leads to full hugs, which leads to small kisses, which leads to passionate kissing, which leads to petting, which leads to clothes being taken off. You get my drift. How far would you go with Jesus sitting in the room next to you? Ouch! That's hard.

In the past I asked myself, "Sheri, how far would I want my future husband to go with a girl that's not me? Would I want his hands all over her like my boyfriend's arms are all over me? What if there was a magical glass mirror that would allow me to see them in the back of a car kissing passionately? Or worse, what if he could see me? Would he still want to marry me?" Ouch! When we consider our future husbands in the arms of another girl, it's not fun. It's sad to think that another girl is getting a piece of his heart, a piece that should belong to his wife alone! Will there be any left for you and me? Am I giving pieces of my heart away too?

If I could go back in time and live my teenage years all over again, I would save my first kiss for my husband Tony. Instead I gave it to a guy in seventh grade outside a school dance. How stupid and shallow was that? I continued to give kisses away to a few other guys before my husband. I am thankful for the Lord's mercy though, in giving me Christian boyfriends who respected me and themselves enough to set up boundaries.

As I look back, I can't even remember those shallow kisses and hugs. But I know they happened and I wish I had saved them all for Tony. Our Father is merciful and I praise him for giving me a passion to remain pure. I pray for you to have the same passion. For when your wedding night comes, sister, I know you'll be thankful that you stood the test. You see, my husband was a love worth waiting for. Yours will be to.

The Man of Your Dreams

In the last chapter we talked about the fact that a super model realizes love is worth waiting for. True love, that is. Have you ever stopped to think that before you are a bride on this earth, you are the bride of heaven?

> "Let us celebrate, let us rejoice, let us give him the glory! The Marriage of the Lamb has come; his Wife has made herself ready. She was given a bridal gown of bright and shining linen. The linen is the righteousness of the saints."
>
> *Revelation 19:7 and 8 The Message*

Jesus should be the true man of our dreams, sister. There is no guy on the planet that can make us feel the way he does. Someday, if you do marry, your husband will be thankful that Jesus was the first man you dreamed about. When Jesus comes first, everything else falls into place.

With Jesus as the man of our dreams, our standards for dating stay HIGH! It is pretty hard to keep our focus on Christ and give our hearts away to lowlife losers. Don't you think?

Below, I have listed some of the reasons Jesus should be the man of our dreams. As you read my list, think about adding some more reasons of your own.

1. He never leaves me - not to work, to run errands, to attend a football game, to go hunting, or anywhere!
2. He loves me unconditionally with no strings attached.
3. He always wants the best for me.
4. He is always praying for me, interceding to the Father on my behalf.
5. He doesn't change.
6. He is patient with me under all circumstances.
7. He heals me when I'm sick.
8. He provides everything I need.
9. Every good and perfect gift is from him.
10. I lack nothing when he's around.
11. He leads me and guides me through all steps of life.
12. He will never forget my birthday, my favorite color, or even my favorite food.
13. He always thinks I'm beautiful.
14. He gave his life for mine.
15. He wants to know my thoughts and will listen to me ramble on and on about my day.
16. He has written me the longest, most perfect love letter on earth - The Word.
17. He won't dump me because another girl makes him laugh or is prettier than I am.

18. He thinks only good thoughts about me.

Can you think of some more reasons why Jesus is the man of your dreams?

There is no man that can replace him. I believe that the Lord provides earthly men like our dads, our husbands, and our brothers to model Christ's love for us. The fact is, though, that they *will* make mistakes. They aren't perfect like our Savior Jesus Christ.

I can't say that I always waited patiently for my husband. There were times I got off track and simply wanted the attention and affection of a guy. Flirting took over at school, youth groups, and the mall. My flesh got in the way and I would ask the Lord why it was taking so long to meet the right one. It was easy to start praying for a young man and end up daydreaming about going out on a date, looking into his eyes, and leaning in for a romantic kiss. Sometimes I just didn't feel complete unless I had the attention of a guy. During those confused and misdirected moments I often felt God gently take my hand and lead me to a place of understanding. I made a decision to be patient. It was a daily choice, a decision to be disciplined and use wisdom. I had to remember that God sees the bigger picture. He knows my future.

> *"So there is hope for your future," declares the Lord.*
>
> *Jeremiah 31:17a*

One of the biggest lessons the Lord has taught me since I have been married is that my precious husband, as wonderful as he is, can never make me feel like Jesus does. My husband loves me, but he isn't perfect. I'm not either. When my focus gets off Jesus, I start to think Tony should provide for my *every* need. I get let down, sometimes even hurt. Like the day I felt sick (it was that time of the month) and I growled at Tony when he got home from work, "You never tell me I'm beautiful! Why are you ignoring me today?"

Tony smiled and said, "Sweetheart, I do love you. You are totally overreacting. I just got home from work. Give me a minute to get my shorts on and then I'll come talk to you about your day."

While he was in our bedroom changing, God reminded me that Tony did in fact kiss me, tell me he loved me and that I was beautiful before he left for work that morning. Oh, I felt so ashamed. I spouted off to my husband because I was feeling bad about myself. It wasn't his fault. It was mine. I didn't go to the Great Comforter to get my comfort. I expected Tony to read my mind and fix my heart. Only Jesus can do that. So when I go to the cross, asking him to fill me up with his love, my husband is free! Tony is free to love me the best that he knows how with God's help. He doesn't feel pressure or like I am sucking the life out of him, because I am going to Christ to meet my needs.

Another way to keep our standards high is to make a list of the things we want in an earthly man of our dreams. Get ready to have some fun!

I went to Hidden Acres Camp when I was fourteen years old and heard one of the speakers talk about how she had made a list of the qualities she wanted in her future husband. As she wrote each quality on a piece of notebook paper she made a decision to pray for her Mr. Right. She kept the list in the outside zipper of her Bible cover and would pray for her future husband every week. She also told us that we have to be a little flexible because God's ways are higher than ours. However, the discipline to pray for our mate was vital to our future happiness. She inspired me, so I too made a list and began praying.

I took her words to heart. As soon as I got home from camp, I started to make my list. I had a blast sitting down and thinking of the qualities that I really wanted *him* to have. It was like making up my own perfect man! I wrote down all kinds of things. I wanted someone who loved the Lord with all his heart, soul, mind, and strength. I wanted a man full of faith and of the Holy Spirit. I wanted a man who loved adventure, other cultures, and travel. I wanted someone who knew who he was in Christ and was not afraid to be different from the world around him. I wanted someone who cared about people and also would love my family. I wanted to marry a man who was strong on the outside, but who was humble on the inside. I wanted to marry a leader. I wanted a man with vision that was not ashamed of the gospel. I wanted a man who loved children and would make a godly father someday to our babies. I wanted to spend my life growing old with a man who had a purpose and passion for life. I wanted a husband who was my very best friend, someone to laugh with! And, I put a little note at the bottom of the page that I would like him to be muscular and handsome! God cares about everything, right?

From the day I finished my list of 25 qualities, I began to pray for this man. I can't help but believe that my prayers played a big part in my husband's life. They still do!

What kind of person do you want to marry? What kind of character qualities do you want him to have? Honesty? Integrity? Purity? Self-control? Intelligence? Be specific.

You see, God is preparing a man that is just right for you and at the same time he is preparing you for that man. I laugh when I read some of the notes my husband Tony wrote me during our engagement time:

> "You are a complete blessing from God, Sheri Riley. He knew what I wanted and sent it to me with additional blessings! When God gave me you, he gave me everything I ever prayed for and then some! It's kind of like a glazed doughnut. You ask for a homemade fresh glazed doughnut all your life, and then God spends years making this fresh doughnut you asked for. When it's finally prepared, he gives you the doughnut fresh, hot, steamy, great, and delicious, but as an added bonus he throws in the sweet little candy sprinkles on top! Awesome. You are my doughnut with extra sweet candies sprinkled on top. And I love you with all of my heart!"

Okay, you might be laughing, but at the time it was the sweetest example to me of how God prepares us for our mates.

Take some time away from reading now and make a list of our own. Have fun, but take it seriously. Really pray about what kind of man you want to marry.

Most importantly, begin to pray for him. Pray for him at least once a week and you will be amazed what the Lord will do!

> "The prayer of a righteous man (woman) is powerful and effective."
> JAMES 5:16B

When you have made a commitment to the Lord to keep your standards high, you won't be disappointed. Your future marriage will be based on the Word of God, not on the characteristics that this world says are important - the body, money, status, and personality. It makes me so angry to see how Hollywood portrays marriage. It's all about sex, tight clothes, and rock-hard bodies. Many of our so-called role models get married and divorced over and over again. Some do this without thinking twice, because their love is all based on status and the *outside*.

Tommy Nelson, in his study "Song of Solomon," says this about finding the mate God has for you: "A person looking for a mate is like running on a track. The track is a personal relationship with Jesus Christ. The goal of the race is to become more like Christ. As we run we will see others running the race as well. When a person is running, he will see another running the same pace he is. After a while, one might say, 'Hey, let's run a lap or two together and see what it is like.' In time, the man will say at some point, 'We are both running the same race, the race for Christ. Why don't we run the race together?' Finding a mate is not a race unto itself. *It is something that naturally happens when we run God's race.*"

Sister, if you are running God's race he will bring you to your mate. In Genesis, when God created Adam, he didn't tell him to go looking all over creation for Eve. He didn't have to date twenty women to find the perfect match. And he certainly didn't have to "try her out" before becoming her husband. You see, God brought Eve to Adam. She was God's perfectly custom-made helpmate for Adam. The *woman* of his dreams!

The Lord can do the same for you. In the meantime, your goal is to run the race for Christ. Be that woman of beautiful character and virtue that a godly man *will want* to run alongside him for a lifetime.

A Divine Fairytale

> ".…. All the days ordained for me were written in your book before one of them came to be."
>
> Psalm 139:16

This is one of the most exciting chapters on the road to being a super model. In the last two chapters we have talked about purity, sexual abstinence, waiting for your mate, and letting God use your life powerfully ways while you're still single.

Most of you will get married some day though. The thought of my future wedding day made me so excited that I wanted to look through all the bridal magazines on Barnes & Noble's shelves! As a little girl I would look at my parents ornate wedding album and dream of the enchanted moment that my prince charming would take me away to his castle. I gazed at how beautiful my mom was in her satin wedding gown and stared at her diamond wedding band as though it were the most precious stone on earth. My imagination would take me into the future, the day that I too would walk down a church aisle in a magnificent white gown. There would be fragrant roses of all colors and sizes lavishly decorating the room and a delicate harp would play a wedding melody that made the heavens open.

One of my girlfriends, came over to my house after school one night. She was two years younger than me, but one of my closest sisters in the Lord. She sparkled with the love of God. She was always one of the first to pray for someone or find a way to serve others to show them Jesus. One of the other reasons I admired her was for her heart for missions. She did and still has a passion to reach the world with the saving news of Jesus Christ. That night my friend came bouncing into my house with a radiant kind of joy that I had never seen before! It took me back because she was joyful all the time any ways. But this was different. She sat on my bed and began to share with me the story of how she met the man she was going to marry at a youth retreat or something like that. She just *knew* he was "the one." He had asked her dad if he could court her and prepare for marriage in the future. The young man had also agreed not to kiss her until their wedding day. The light in my friend's eyes as she talked almost made me cry. I was so happy for her. I loved hearing all the sweet details of their courtship and began praying for them daily.

A few months later my dear friend shared with me that she had "missed" God. She had heard wrong. This guy was not "the one". I'm not sure what happened, exactly. I do know it was a pure situation, but that they completely broke off their courtship.

I have to chuckle a bit when I think back to those days now. That same joyful girlfriend of mine is married to a wonderful godly man, serving in youth ministry together. I also laugh because of the three other guys in my life I thought I might marry before I met my husband Tony. One of the guys I dated for two and a half years, another was a close friend that I had known my whole life, and another was someone I didn't know very well, but respected a great deal. I guess I never thought "for sure" I would marry any of those guys, but I definitely thought about it and talked about it at times. It's a natural feeling to have, but I sure wish I had saved every feeling for my future husband.

One of my high school basketball teammates said recently, "I wish I would have kept my kisses, hugs, love, and dreams for my fiancé Adam. He is getting my whole heart and my whole body, but I wasted so much time and so many thoughts on my high school boyfriend."

I agree with her. In one sense I am thankful for those relationships because I learned a lot and the Lord used those situations to make me into the woman I am today. I have seen in a very real way that God redeems our time and has a very special plan for all his little girls.

Hollywood

Often times as young women we don't believe God has a love story created for us. We don't believe that he is working everything out for our good. I mean everything! (Romans 8:28) When our latest immature and obnoxious crush breaks our heart, we wonder if we will ever recover? We reason that we were more in-love with the idea of being in-love, than we were with the boy himself. It still hurts though. The pain is real. It's like putting your heart through a meat grinder and expecting it to come out without a scratch.

We look to Hollywood and various teen idols that seem to have it all together in their fairytale lives. They appear so happy, so rich, and so in-love.

Girl, you are not alone in your struggle. It is hard to see past the world's glare to realize that if God plans for us to marry, his true love will put what Hollywood has to utter shame! So, I pray that you would overcome your desire to have a Hollywood romance of your own. I pray that you would let God write your love story. A divine fairytale that only the author of creation could script.

Love stories

My cousin John and his wife Kristi's story begin with a phone call. They were introduced through mutual friends while attending colleges in Oklahoma and Texas. Their romance endured over six years as they went through college, graduated, and started their careers. John as an engineer and Kristi as a school-teacher. God fashioned a love story of patients and perseverance made just for them. He has honored their obedience. When people meet them today, they can see that after eight years of marriage, their love is alive and deep. They have three adorable children and are a testimony that true love is only found through Christ. The author of creation has scripted John and Kristi's story.

I have also been told the story of a businessman, having lunch in a restaurant while trying to get the phone number of one of the pretty waitresses. The man did eventually get her phone number, they went out several times, fell in-love, got married, and had a baby girl three years later. That baby girl happens to be me!

Whether God plans for us to be single, to meet our husbands in college, at a restaurant, or in a far away land, if you and my love stories are written by the King of Kings, each story will be a divine fairytale!

Mr. Egypt meets Miss Iowa

Five years ago I began to fast and pray for three months about my future husband. I was confused about a guy I liked. I prayed and earnestly felt called to spend a few months alone with the Lord, seeking His will about my future. Some days I would fast from food, some from TV, and even did what I have heard referred to as "A Daniel Fast," (Daniel 1:8-21) eating only raw fruits, vegetables, and water for days at a time. Mostly though I just fasted from talking to that particular young man, focusing completely on Christ. By the time those three months of fasting were over I knew that I was exactly where the Lord wanted me to be. Single that is!

Just one week after my fasting period was over I was at a meeting with my friend Kristie. It was a business conference in Louisville, Kentucky, in March of 1999. Kristie had brought with her a girl from one of our Bible studies named Heidi. For no particular reason they started to get silly, laughing and joking with me saying, "Sheri, we are going to get you married! We know who your husband will be!" I laughed too, just because I thought they were both crazy! Honestly though, I don't think either of them were prepared for what happened next. God was using their joke to bring me to my husband who neither one of them had ever met or talked to.

Heidi had given my phone number to a friend of hers. A kind, godly woman named Linda Prescott, who was living in Texas. Linda had an adventurous son named James Anthony Prescott, who they called Tony, who was working for the United Nations, training UN troops in Sharm El Sheik, Egypt. Heidi and Linda had talked on the phone and through their conversations thought Tony and I would enjoy getting to know each other. They gave Tony my phone number and told him that a former Miss Iowa wanted him to call her. (I didn't know anything about this part.) A few days later my telephone rang at 6:00AM in the morning. I heard it ringing, but decided that whoever it was could leave a message because I was tired from a night spent helping my friend Tracy with her upcoming wedding plans.

If I had known who was calling I would have jumped out of my cozy comforter immediately! I really just thought this Tony Prescott guy was not a real person or if he was real, Heidi was still just being insane. I never thought he would actually call me. Especially from Egypt.

A few hours later on that cold March morning, I checked my answering machine. Much to my surprise there was a warm, strong voice on the other end of the phone. It was Tony Prescott! I was in shock! I wanted this Tony man to be true, but I honestly thought nothing would come of it. I was wrong. He was a *very* real person. He was eight and a half years older than me, was raised in a small town outside of Ft. Worth, Texas, and gave his heart to Jesus when he was a little boy.

Several hours passed that morning when the phone rang again. This time I rushed over to my dresser to answer it! It was that same warm, manly voice that I had listened to over a dozen times on my machine that morning. This time we were able to talk - a talk that lasted over one hour. I can't even remember what we talked about. Just in general questions I think. Like; "What are you doing in Egypt?" "How is life in Iowa?" "Is that where you grew up?" "Tell me a little about yourself." In that one hour I knew enough that I desperately wanted to talk to Tony again. I had butterflies in my stomach! He left me his number and address, saying we would keep in touch.

Tony and I did stay in touch. We talked every day from then on for over two weeks. When I told Kristie and Heidi about our phone calls they were shocked. They couldn't believe what was happening!

I shared every detail with my parents from the first day Tony called. I told them that I thought he was "the one." I had never met him and had seen only a picture faxed to me by his mother. It was blurry and dark. He hadn't seen a picture of me at this point either. I somehow knew though that this was the man God had been preparing for me even before I was born. The Lord knew exactly what I needed and had been orchestrating our every move. My parents did caution me, saying that marriage is wonderful and ordained by God, but that doesn't make it easy. It's hard work to have a healthy, loving, godly relationship. They shared with me that Tony and I would face trials and struggles just like every couple. Especially because our courtship began while living 5000 miles apart. However, if it was God's will, what He joined together, no man could separate.

During that second week of talking on the phone we both received letters and pictures of each other in the mail. My hands almost shook as I opened the envelope with Egyptian postal stamps on it. I gazed at each picture of Tony and had to pinch myself to believe that this was really happening. He was so handsome! He was about 5'10" and had dark hair with blond highlights that had been bleached from the sun and the Red Sea. His blue eyes sparkled. Tony was appealing inside and out. But, It's what's inside that lasts.

I learned about his heart from hours of talking on the phone. I was blessed to hear him share about his love for the Lord and how he had seen God's hand protect and guide him through the twenty-nine years that he had spent on the earth. I learned that Moses was his favorite Bible character and that he had a love for learning other languages. He took joy in becoming familiar with other cultures too. He spoke Italian fluently and had a working knowledge in Arabic and Russian. He had already traveled to more places than I could ever dream. Russia, Italy, France, Spain, Germany, Israel, and Jordan. He grew up in Texas, where his dad coached him in little league baseball and taught him to hunt. He had three sisters and a mom that loved to spoil them with her cooking! Tony wasn't perfect (of course) and he shared his past struggles with me too. We were honest with each other and I know that the Lord honored our truthfulness. We had many things in common, but many differences too. Today, it's the differences that cause us to grow.

> *"God wants us to grow up, to know the whole truth and tell it in love – like Christ in everything. We take our lead from Christ who is the source of everything we do. He keeps us in step with each other. His very breath and blood flow through us, nourishing us so that we will grow up healthy in God, robust in love."*
>
> EPHESIANS 4:15&16 THE MESSAGE

When we talked on the phone for those two weeks each time we were done with a conversation and had to hang up the phone, I caught myself wanting to say, "I miss you" or "I love you." How could I miss someone that I had never met? And, how could I love someone I hadn't seen? It was strange, yet completely natural and normal at the time. Tony was feeling the same way. As I prayed for him and about him I could feel the Holy Spirit reaffirming what I knew in my spirit to be true. This man on the other side of the world was the man that I was going to spend my life serving the Lord with. For sure. I had no doubts.

When those two weeks were coming to an end, Tony asked me if I would like to come to Egypt to meet him. Our phone bills had become monstrous, and he wasn't able to come to the States at that time. We prayed and our family's prayed.

I need to make a note here that this was a *very* unusual circumstance. For the most part, I can't imagine recommending another young woman to follow my lead. Especially now that Tony and I have a daughter, I can't imagine how much faith my parents must have had? It seams very un-safe and strange to say the least. I can't put into words though how "right" it was. I also want to remind you before you go running off to other countries to meet people or just down the road for that matter, make sure that the spiritual mentors in your life agree with you. My parents would not have let their 20 year old daughter go if they hadn't have trusted the Lord, me, and Tony. They knew that they had nothing to worry about because the Lord had given them his peace. By faith they accepted His plan. I also asked my pastor and his wife for wise counsel. In addition I would *strongly* recommend that you do not meet men over the internet or through chat rooms. This could be very un-safe. Remember that the Lord moves in mysterious ways, but we need to use wisdom and discernment.

The Sunday morning before I left for the Middle East, I was in church. At this point I hadn't told *anyone* but Kristie and Heidi, about going to see Tony in

Egypt. That Sunday morning I went up to the front of our church for prayer. I felt a gentle hand on my back. A woman who I didn't know began to prophesy over my life. She said, "I am not sure why I am telling you this. I don't even know you. But, I feel like the Lord wants me to tell you that your husband is going to come to you in a very supernatural way. It is going to happen quickly and most people won't understand." I felt the hand leave my back and didn't meet that woman until several months later.

I was shaking and realized that the Lord was confirming once again what I knew in my spirit to be true. Tony was going to be my husband through a very supernatural kind of circumstance. It was happening quickly and for sure, most people wouldn't understand a story like ours.

The day before I left I for Egypt, I called my best friend, Kelli, in Oklahoma. The weeks had flown by and I hadn't told her about Tony yet. When I did speak with her, she already knew what I was going to say. The Lord had confirmed it in her spirit also. Again I was shocked! How did she know? She had been praying for me, was overjoyed, and felt blessed to be a part of this miracle. I think the Lord was showing her too, that He could do anything. Nothing is impossible for Him!

Egypt here I come

The day had arrived. I woke up early to take a shower and make sure everything was packed. I certainly didn't want to forget anything. It wasn't like there was going to be a Wal-Mart to run to for a tube of toothpaste in Egypt. My parents had to go out of town on business so my friends Kristie and Heidi drove me to the airport and walked with me to the international boarding terminal where we said our good-byes. I think we were all in awe of the magnitude of what was taking place.

The flight was long over the Pacific Ocean. I slept a lot, read my Bible, and chatted with a few of the other passengers to make the time pass. I really wasn't nervous as the flight attendant said in four different languages that we had landed in Cairo, Egypt. I walked through the long steal corridor and out into the crowded airport. I looked back and forth through the hundreds of Egyptian nationals and then I heard that familiar voice say, "Sheri!" Our eyes met for the first time. He gently took my arm, leading me out of the crowd of people and over to the taxi we would take to our hotel. The next thing I knew we were sitting in the back of an Egyptian cab together. We both couldn't believe that we were really sitting next to the person we had grown to love over the phone during those past three weeks.

After a few minutes we arrived at the elegant resort hotel where we would be staying. Tony escorted me to my room realizing that I needed to relax and freshen up before going to dinner.

As he went down the hallway to his room I collapsed on my soft new bed in Egypt. The hotel room looked different than any I had ever stayed in before. It was modern, yet with a Middle Eastern flair of course. It was comfortable and exciting as I opened my suitcase to decide what to wear for our first dinner together. It almost didn't seam real. I had to pinch myself! Had I really just met my future husband in person?

Tony walked to my room a few hours later, gave me a huge smile and warm hug. We walked around the hotel laughing and talking as if we had known each other our whole lives. We ended up at a restaurant in the hotel, being seated at a candle lit table overlooking the atrium. Tony ordered dinner for us and we held hands across the white linen tablecloth. The night air was warm and the lights shown softly throughout the room. When our food came Tony prayed and thanked our heavenly Father for bringing us together. He thanked the Lord for me and asked him to bless our time together in Egypt, to make it pleasing in his sight… I almost cried.

We spent a few more days in Cairo and then we boarded another plane to fly to the Sinai Peninsula, where Tony had been working for the past three years. It was a flourishing resort town called Sharm El Sheik, located right on the Red Sea and a United Nations Base is located there. I could go on and on about our adventures in Egypt: the camel ride through the ancient pyramids, snorkeling in the Red Sea, our conversations over authentic dinners, shopping in the crowded markets, and deep sea fishing for tuna-fish. All of it seems like a far off dream now, but it all happened. Those ten days I spent in Egypt with my future husband were more romantic and special than I could have ever prayed for. And, the pictures we took in Egypt, we now have displayed in our home and have fond memories of the first time we met in person.

I flew back to the United States knowing that I would be married soon. Tony and I asked the Lord to show us his perfect timing while we wrote letters and talked on the phone.

Tony finished his work for the United Nations almost one month after I arrived home in Iowa. After praying through various job opportunities, Tony knew the Lord was telling him to move back to America and marry me! I was more than excited about his decision and eagerly awaited the time I could share him with my parents, family, and friends. When that opportunity came they loved him. He fit into our family as though he had always been a part of it. They certainly didn't agree on everything, but the similarities outweighed the differences. Soon after asking my dad if he could have my hand in marriage, both of our families were in Arlington, Texas, spending time getting better acquainted. Tony "officially" proposed to me beside Lake Arlington. All I can honestly remember is Tony getting down on one knee as I began to cry. He put a sparkling diamond engagement ring on my left hand and asked me be his wife. Of course I said yes!

The "big day"

We planned on getting married five months from the date of our engagement, in my hometown of Clear Lake, Iowa. We tried to see each other as often as we could. It was difficult because Tony had started working in Denver, Colorado, and I was still in Iowa, with my family planning our wedding.

During those months Tony had some issues come up with his family that caused a large amount of stress for him. He even considered postponing our wedding to work through the struggles. We also had conflicts about where we were headed and what our goals were for our future together. There even came a day that we wrestled with the idea of canceling our marriage plans all together. We were feeling stress and Satan was trying to destroy God's plans by planting doubt in our hearts.

> *"Be self-controlled and alert. Your enemy the devil prowls around like a roaring lion looking for someone to devour."*
>
> 1 Peter 5:8

We had pre-marital counseling with my pastor Dave a few times over the phone and once in person. It was refreshing to pray with him about our future as husband and wife. We learned more about each other and found ways to work through differences and then to enjoy our similarities. When our big day, November 20th, 1999, finally arrived we were more than ready because,

> *"Love is patient, love is kind. It does not envy, it does not boast, it is not proud. It is not rude, it is not self-seeking, it is not easily angered, it keeps no record of wrongs. Love does not delight in evil, but rejoices with the truth. It always protects, always trusts, always hopes, always perseveres."*
>
> 1 Corinthians 13:4-7

"I do"

Our wedding was held in a large ballroom called "The Surf." My church was too small for the nine hundred guests that we had invited. It was a large celebration of the Lord's miraculous love and faithfulness. A celebration of divine and miraculous love!

The gospel message was clearly woven through the entire ceremony and reception. All the candles and soft harp music turned out exactly how I imagined them in my dreams as a little girl. The various cream colored roses were breathtaking and the white and gold decorations made the room look like a castle! The Lord gave me more of a glorious wedding than I could have ever asked him for. After we sang to each other, recited our vows, and lit our unity candle our pastor said, "Tony, you may now kiss your bride." In that moment I felt as if I had been Tony's bride my whole life, just waiting for the moment to happen on earth.

We had the traditional cutting of the delicious wedding cake (Tony smeared frosting all over my cheek!), greeted our guests, and had an Italian style reception. That night as we rode off to our honeymoon we praised the Lord for the blessing he had given to us in each other. We reaffirmed privately the commitments we had made to love, honor, and cherish each other for the rest of our lives. As the lyrics of the song I sang to Tony earlier that day said, "I'll live for you, you'll live for me, and we'll live for Him. Through all the years, the laughter and tears, through thick and thin. Faithful and true my love for you will only grow stronger. Because I'll live for you, you'll live for me, and we will live for Him."

Mentors

Who do you admire? I'm not talking about the girls you like to hang out with or your group of friends. I want to know, "Who do you admire?" Is there a woman who makes you think, "Wow. I would love to be like her." Do you have a person you go to for counsel and guidance? Who do you ask for advice when you have questions about dating and sex? Who do you talk to when you wonder if you should give up your dream of going to college? What person do you listen to for guidance when you're questioning God's will about going on a mission trip to Venezuela next summer?

Let me share a secret with you. Lean in close, you don't want to miss this. One of the biggest gifts God has given you and me is older women. I'm not just talking about the ones with white hair and thick glasses. I mean the older women that the Bible talks about in Titus 2:3-5,

> "Likewise, teach older women to be reverent in the way they live, not to be slanders or addicted to much wine, but to teach what is good. Then they can teach the younger women to love their husbands and children, to be self-controlled and pure, to be busy at home, to be kind, and to be subject to their husbands, so that no one will malign the word of God."

My dad's parents lived in Dallas, Texas, for most of my young life. We were only able to see them a few times a year. A memory I cherish is traveling down south to celebrate Christmas with my Riley grandparents. A highlight of the season was making sugar cookies in a variety of holiday shapes and frosting them in thick green, red, and blue icing. I loved watching my grandmother carefully hold each baked cookie, turning it into a picture that was almost too beautiful to eat. I also remember her setting the table for Christmas dinner with red and green décor. She almost floated around the kitchen, preparing the feast. She had no idea that my little eyes were watching her every move. She was becoming a mentor of mine, teaching me something valuable.

Today as I prepare holiday meals in my home, I remember how my grandmother did things and I want to do the same. This past Christmas season I invited a friend and her young son to our home to decorate holiday cookies. I have to admit that mine didn't turn out as well as my grandmother's, but I'm sure they will improve with time.

Can you think of a woman who has made a difference in your life? She may have taught you something simple, like preparing a box of macaroni and cheese, or it may have been something life changing, like leading you to Christ. God puts these women in our lives for a specific reason.

For most of us, our first teachers are our moms. They are our first mentors. If our moms are not Christians or are not involved in our lives, God will provide someone else. He will give us older women to fill in where our earthly mother may be unable or unwilling. I call these women "spiritual mothers." These spiritual mothers may come in the form of a grandmother, a youth pastor, a school teacher, a track coach, a voice teacher, or even a hairstylist! Keep your eyes open—she could be anywhere!

A close friend of mine is a high school teacher. She shared with me that when she listens to her students talk, they rarely mention their parents. They care more about what their friends and MTV think about life than what their moms believe. That may be the culture you and I live in today, but I don't believe that's what God intended for us as young women. Friends are great and important. It is wonderful to have a friend to have fun with, to laugh and to play with. It is great to have friends to share the comfort of companionship with, but we need mentors too.

Mike Murdock, the author of *The Three Most Important Things in Your Life*, says, "A friend loves you the way you are, but a mentor loves you too much to leave you the way you are."

Sis, a mentor is a priceless person who causes you to want to be more than you are right now. They will challenge you and guide you. A mentor may not be your favorite person because change hurts. However, your mentor will mean more to you in the long run than hundreds of friends who accept mediocrity in your life.

"Listen, my son, to your father's instruction
and do not forsake your mother's teaching."
PROVERBS 1:8

King Solomon was the wisest man who ever lived. In one of his first proverbs he cautions you and I not to forsake our mother's teaching. He probably knew that we wouldn't always agree with our mothers, nor should we all the time. If our mother wants to give us birth-control pills to insure we don't get pregnant, we shouldn't agree with her. We should remind her of our commitment to abstinence – nothing else is safe! Or if our mother asks us to lie for her, of course we should not. You see, God gave us mothers that should teach us principles that direct and guide us as we grow from babies into women. For that reason, I believe it's critical that we develop good relationships with our moms.

Our moms teach us practical lessons, like how to mix a box of brownies and how to apply lip-gloss, but it's the matters of the heart that are most important. Moms provide the skills and life lessons that will last for eternity. Your mom might be the first woman you heard pray or saw open her Bible. Your mom might have been the first person to help you understand the salvation message. Your mom might have been the one who helped you reach your first goal or realize your first dream. She may have been the person you watched treat others with kindness, so in turn you treated your friends at the park with kindness. Whether your mentor is your biological mother or not, you are blessed that God has placed her in your life.

Do you yell at your mom often, screaming your head off and stomping into the other room when you don't agree with her? Would you rather she get out of your face and stay away from your business? Honestly, my friend, that is sin. Rebellion is sin. One way that Satan will crack a hole in our lives is by creating a wedge between our moms and us. When I observe many other young women, I see that unfortunately he's doing a good job of it right now. Don't get me wrong; I know moms aren't perfect. I love my mom with all my heart and she's my greatest mentor, but we don't agree on everything. I do respect and honor her, though. I don't lash out at her, cutting her down. She has feelings. So does your mom. You are able to hurt your mom just as badly as you are convinced that she's hurting you. So strive for peace! Sit down and have a heart-to-heart with your mom. Tell her that you want to be close to her and you are willing to try to understand her. She wants to understand you, too. Communicate. Pray together. Ask God to teach you all he can during your short time at home with your parents. God puts us in their care long enough to protect us and guide us until we can be out on our own. They are appointed to teach us to fly, then to let us go.

The truth is that our moms have already been around the block a time or two. They have made mistakes and don't want us to fall in the same pits. They have also succeeded at many things and it's time we listened to their stories! Pastor Terry Wilkinson teaches, "A wise man (young woman) learns from other's mistakes, but the wisest man learns from other's successes!"

Lies

Satan has lied, encouraging us to base our actions on what the world says we should do. He says, "You need to take care of you, don't worry about anyone else." "The only way to be happy is to be a feminist. Men are puppets on a string." "Your body is your own. Do whatever feels good." "Tolerate everything and everyone." "Sex sells, so be sexy!" Unfortunately, many of us have chosen role models like Christina Aguilera, Jennifer Lopez, and Halle Berry. These women may mean well, but they are polluting our hearts and minds. You see, *wrong is wrong* even if everyone does it and *right is right* even if no one does it.

The majority of Hollywood stars and music divas should not be our standard for right and wrong. Divorce is a sin even if they paint it as necessary and acceptable. Sex before marriage is a sin even if they portray it as romantic and fulfilling. Selfishness is a sin even if they try to make us believe women need to stand up for themselves. Dancing while doing gestures that look like masturbation is sin even if music videos are supposed to be just entertainment and fun.

> *"The world and its desires will pass away, but the man who does the will of God lives forever."*
>
> *1 John 2:17*

There *are* people in the spotlight, though, who can be great role models for us as young women. Corrie Ten Boom, who wrote *The Hiding Place*, tells her experiences as a Christian in a Nazi concentration camp. Mother Theresa became a servant to those on our earth that lived without the comforts of food and shelter. Can you think of more? We also have role models living today, like the ladies of the Christian pop music group Point of Grace, our First Lady Laura Bush, or Pam Stenzel, a prominent speaker on sexual purity. How about Kirk Cameron's beautiful wife Chelsea Noble? There are a whole slew of other godly recording artists that I could mention. We need to open our eyes to find these women!

There are others that may not wear a crown or have their name in lights, but should be our role models. Who do you respect for reaching great heights in her professional career? Is there a woman you believe deserves a gold metal for being a fantastic mom? Do you know someone who has overcome great odds or not given up under horrifying circumstances? Who has made an impact on your life by the way they live theirs?

The next step

Now that we have identified *who* our mentors should be, where do we go from here? We are blessed to have mentors, but we must be *willing* to be taught. We can surround ourselves with godly women of faith, yet not learn anything if our hearts aren't teachable. Are you ready to be counseled and discipled? God may be waving mentors right in our faces, but we are too stubborn to look. We can be such proud know-it-alls, can't we? If we humble ourselves and listen to our mentor's teaching, we will succeed in life! Just as our nation's president needs to seek guidance from his cabinet, we will only grow wise with the right advisors surrounding us.

> "For lack of guidance a nation falls, but many advisers make victory sure."
> PROVERBS 11:14

> *"Plans fail for lack of counsel, but with many advisers they succeed."*
> PROVERBS *15:22*

> *"He who walks with the wise grows wise, but a companion of fools suffers harm."*
> PROVERBS *13:20*

Let's look closer at Titus' description of older women teaching us…

1. *She will teach us what is good.* Boy, I could write a whole chapter on what is good. But the best example I can think of is in Proverbs 31:30, "*Charm is deceptive and beauty is fleeting, but a woman who fears the Lord is to be praised.*" She is the good woman. She knows that beauty on the outside will fade. It's only what's on the inside that will last. That is what counts for eternity.

2. *She will teach us to love our husbands and children.* A husband and children may be the furthest subject from your mind right now. What I want you to realize is that the

way you treat your dad, mom, brothers and sisters today, is how you will treat your husband and children tomorrow. We are creating patterns of behavior at this very moment that will affect the rest of our lives, and our future families. Today you are making a choice to be an excellent wife or a terrible wife. Today you are making a choice to be a selfish mother or a selfless mother.

Our mentor should be a woman who builds her husband up, not tears him down with degrading words. She doesn't nag or try to rule with an iron fist. She praises, submits, and loves. She is also a woman who gives sacrificially to her children, teaching them to serve the Lord. She is more concerned with blessing her family than being blessed herself. Begin to pray that any stronghold regarding your future husband and children will be broken now. Don't wait.

3. *She will teach us to be self-controlled and pure*. Pick a mentor that practices what she preaches. We will see self-control in her life by the peaceful way she makes choices, how she doesn't worry needlessly, and how she has control over her tongue. We will see Jesus in her! *"Blessed are the pure in heart, for they will see God." Matthew 5:8*

Our mentor may teach us self-control through discipline too. We may want to kick and scream, but it's for our good. *"No discipline seems pleasant at the time, but painful.*

Later on, however, it produces a harvest or righteousness and peace for those who have been trained by it." Hebrews 12:11

4. *She will teach us to be busy at home and to be kind.* I believe that when God created Eve to be Adam's helper, he was visually showing us that our most important job some day as women will be just that – to be our husband's helpmate. The greatest fruit from this will come when we (those of us who get married) consider taking care of him, our children, and our home our highest calling. We need to start praying about this while we're young! "*A wife of noble character is her husband's crown, but a disgraceful wife is like decay in his bones.*" Proverbs 12:4

Even now though, before we become wives and mothers, we can practice being busy at home. We can start by organizing our own bedrooms, cleaning our hairspray and make-up off the bathroom sink, and baking a cake for a friend's birthday. We can take an interest in our sibling's hobbies and be the one to come up with a family game night of activities once a month. We could also go over to our grandparent's homes and volunteer to vacuum, dust, or do their dishes.

As single women we may have people over for dinner – maybe start a "dinner club" where each month you pick a different cuisine to try? One month everyone brings an Italian dish and the next month they bring a Spanish dish. We could have friends over to make care-packages for missionaries or invite other singles over to play games and cheer on our favorite NBA team. We might learn new hobbies like scrap booking or crocheting, inviting our girlfriends over to participate. We could invite our friends over for a "facial night." Have them bring their favorite skin-care and clay masks. We might also consider taking turns with other girls in our youth group, having our youth pastor drop his children off at our homes. He and his wife can go out for a date while we baby-sit their children. We could facilitate a bible study or prayer group in our homes too! We should start right now by being helpmates to our parents, siblings, and friends, all the while preparing our hearts to be busy at home in the future.

The world has painted the stay-at-home mom as boring, uneducated, and worthless. That is a giant lie! The women that stay at home and choose to raise their children many times have multiple degrees. They are educated through books and their hobbies, they understand current events, and they always have something to do. They can be the most interesting, fascinating women you will ever meet. I pray that as you dream about a career and reach for your educational goals, you won't forget to make a home life your first priority. Don't let your work and ambitions outside your home ruin your husband and children, making them feel unworthy, unloved, neglected, and a burden.

I recently read Dr. Laura Schlessinger's best-selling book *The Proper Care & Feeding of Husbands.* She writes, "If you decide that the most important thing about your life is your worker-ant role, you'll likely feel drained a lot of the time and resent the obligations you have to your husband and children – obligations that, ironically, will save you from that feeling of being drained in the first place. Check out all the competitive backbiting, layoffs, and computerization and mechanization substitutions for human beings going on in the workplace. Meanwhile, you are a goddess to your children and a queen to your husband. Aside from the paycheck issue, which one is more nourishing and rewarding?"

She continues, "Now let me make something completely clear. I am not suggesting married women should not work. I am not suggesting that there is no valid form of personal expression of creativity and special gifts outside the home. Obviously, I have a radio and writing career. I just took up sailing. I love taking on challenges and doing service. But from day one, I have always made it clear to everyone, especially my husband and child, that if anything got in the way of family, it would get tempered or excises. It's one thing to have a tiring, stressful day – or even week. It's another thing to allow outside activities, no matter how seemingly important, to routinely get in the way of obligations to the roles created by holy vows, moral obligations, and love."

Dear super model, check your priorities with your mentor. Ask her to be honest with you. Let her pray for you. Pray, asking the Lord to make you one of those rare young women who realizes that all the glitz and glimmer of this world won't compare to the love and satisfaction of being a woman busy at home.

I pray that you and I would choose admirable mentors. I pray that we will look for godly role models to help lead and guide us closer to our Savior. I hope you will find, as I have, that your mentors will become some of the most valuable people in your life. And just think – some day, maybe even today, you are being a mentor too.

"Some people enter our lives and leave almost instantly, others stay, and forge such an impression on our heart and soul, we are forever changed." – Author Unknown

Dreams

"Joseph, a young man of seventeen, was tending the flocks with his bothers, the sons of Bilhah and the sons of Zilpah, his father's wives, and he brought their father a bad report about them.

Now Israel (Jacob) loved Joseph more than any of his other sons, because he was born to him in his old age; and he made a richly ornamented robe for him. When his brothers saw that their father loved him more than any of them, they hated him and could not speak a kind word to him.

Joseph had a dream, and when he told it to his brothers, they hated him all the more. He said to them, 'Listen to this dream I had: We were binding sheaves of grain out in the field when suddenly my sheaf rose and stood upright, while your sheaves gathered around mine and bowed down to it.'

> His brothers said to him, 'Do you intend to reign over us? Will you actually rule us?' And they hated him all the more because of his dream and what he had said.
> Then he had another dream, and he told it to his brothers. 'Listen,' he said, 'I had another dream, and this time the sun and moon and eleven stars were bowing down to me.'
>
> GENESIS 37:2-9

A few verses further Joseph's brothers call out to him,

> *"Here comes the dreamer!" they said to each other.*
>
> GENESIS 37:19

The story goes on to give an account of what happens to Joseph over the next several years of his life. His brothers sold him into slavery and he eventually ended up in Egypt. I can't imagine having brothers so evil. I have gotten on my brother's nerves before, but he doesn't hate me!

Because of Joseph's pure character and positive attitude, he was soon accepted into the home of a man named Potiphar, who was one of Pharaoh's officials, the captain of the guard. God prospered young Joseph there and gave him great favor. Later on, though, because Joseph would not sleep with Potiphar's wife when she came on to him, she lied and told her husband that Joseph tried pressuring her to have sex with him. It's sad to see that Joseph made the right choice, yet he was imprisoned because Potiphar didn't believe him. It was thirteen years later before Joseph began to see the dreams that God had given him coming true.

The Pharaoh of Egypt was having some pretty bizarre dreams. They frightened him terribly and he wanted to know what they meant. One of Pharaoh's chief cupbearers had had a dream that was interpreted by Joseph. He told Pharaoh that Joseph might be able to the same for him. Through another series of events Pharaoh, like Potiphar once did, also sees Joseph's character and positive attitude – the hand of God on Joseph's life. Pharaoh put Joseph in charge of the whole land of Egypt—a pretty important job! During this time a famine ravished their land and Joseph's brothers, starving, had come to get grain from Egypt. They ended up literally bowing down to the new governor of the land—Joseph. That seventeen-year-old "dreamer" had grown up and had now become a ruler of one of the most powerful lands in the world. Joseph's dreams literally came true because of his obedience to God's call on his life. He never gave up when he was imprisoned for things he didn't do. He became successful in the midst of trials and times of terrible sorrow. They were times of preparation. God had a purpose for Joseph and he allowed Joseph to suffer in order to grow, to become useful in his plan.

Can you think of other people in the Bible whose dreams came true? How about Hannah? Her dream was to have a child. In Biblical times it was a disgrace not to be able to bear children. Even today it is a deep sorrow that many women live with. Hannah dreamed of holding a tiny baby boy in her arms and nursing him, watching as he grew strong. She wanted to smell that fresh infant smell and hold a soft little body against hers. In 1 Samuel 1:10 and 11, Hannah cries out to the Lord. "*In bitterness of soul Hannah wept much and prayed to the Lord. And she made a vow, saying 'O*

Lord Almighty, if you will only look upon your servant's misery and remember me, and not forget your servant but give her a son, then I will give him to the Lord for all the days of his life, and no razor will ever be used on his head.'"

Her dream did come true! God allowed her to conceive and give birth to a beautiful baby boy whom she named Samuel. Hannah did keep her promise, giving him back to the Lord when he was a few years old. He became a divinely ordained leader, judge, and priest in Israel.

The Lord gives us dreams because he knows that without a vision his people will perish. If we don't have a goal or dream to run after, we will fall by the wayside. Someone once said, "If you don't stand for something, you will fall for anything." If we know the plans that the Lord has for us and we set out to accomplish those plans, we will be amazed at the miracles that will take place before our very eyes. One of my mentors, Sue Cappelan, has said, "Nobody who ever gave her best regretted it!"

What are your dreams? Right now your dream may be to win the next volleyball tournament or come in with the high score at your regional speech meet. You may have a goal to make the cheerleading squad, the basketball team, or the student government. You may want to spend the summer working for your uncle to pay for a new car. You may have a dream to be the valedictorian of your graduating class or maybe your goal is simply to graduate. Possibly you dream about saving enough money for college and getting the scholarship you spent hours writing essays for.

I read a great story in a book called *Expect to Win* by Bill Glass. It reads:

> Back in 1936, Jessie Owens came back from the Olympic Games as the World's Fastest Man. At a huge press conference, the first question asked was, "How did you do it, Jessie? Four gold medals, you embarrassed Hitler in his own hometown, the fastest man in the world...how did you do it?"
>
> "Oh," he said, "I think it all began when I was just a kid back in junior high school, and my coach got us all together and made a speech I've never forgotten. The main thing he said was, 'You can pretty well become whatever you make up your mind to be.'
>
> "As a junior high kid, I looked up at my coach and shouted, 'Coach, I've already decided what I want to be! The fastest man in the world!' And my coach looked down at me, a little skinny, scrawny black boy and said, 'Jessie, that's a great dream. Fact is, Jessie, I don't know if I've ever heard such a great dream like that. There's only one problem with your dream, Jesse.'
>
> "'What's that, coach?'
>
> "'Dreams have a way of floating high in the sky. They just float up there like clouds. Dreams never become realities unless you have the courage to build a ladder to them.'
>
> "'How do you build a ladder to a dream, coach?'
>
> "'Well, Jessie,' he said, 'you build it one step at a time.'"

That story gives me chill bumps. Jessie reached his dream of becoming the fastest man in the world because he focused and never gave up. At a young age he took what his coach said to heart, believing that he could pretty well become whatever he made his mind up to be. You see, a dream is not something that we reach over night. A dream is something that the Lord prepares us for and is realized over time. My mom always told me, "Sheri, you eat an elephant one bite at a time." She is right. A dream takes time to come true, but being young is no excuse not to have one.

Did you know that Einstein wrote his first paper on the theory of relativity at age sixteen? Did you know that Mozart composed his first symphony at age six? King David was anointed the King of Israel at age fifteen and Joan of Arc led 3,000 French Knights to victory at age seventeen! What is your excuse for not going after the dreams God has given you?

I heard one of my dad's friends explaining that it is aerodynamically impossible for the bumblebee to fly. Its body is too heavy and its wings are too small. However, the bumblebee chooses not to be affected by that opinion; he flies, he works, and he achieves.

This world is full of people who start many things but finish very few. We start diets and give up one day when we start craving a piece of greasy pepperoni pizza. We start exercise programs and give up one morning in bed when we are tired and comfortable. We push the snooze button on our alarm clock and drift back to sleep. Many people make a New Year's Resolution to read the Bible from cover to cover, but give up when they miss a day or two. Several ambitious young minds start businesses that never make it past the first year because the trials overwhelm them. They give up too soon. Others of us start playing an instrument but when we want to watch our favorite team play Monday night football, we instantly forget that in order to be in an orchestra some day we must sacrifice leisurely time and commit to practice. So we quit.

God has called us to finish what we start! Timothy says,

> "I have fought the good fight, I have finished the race, I have kept the faith. Now there is in store for me the crown of righteousness, which the Lord, the righteous Judge, will award to me on that day - and not only to me, but also to all who have longed for his appearing."
>
> 2 Timothy 4:7 and 8

Super models finish what they've started. If God gives you a dream, sister, he will give you the strength to finish it!

Miss America

I went to the Miss America Pageant as Miss Iowa 1997-98. At eighteen years old, I had a dream to become Iowa's very first Miss America. I previously shared with you how that dream grew in my heart. I was willing to change, work hard, pray hard, and go forth to finish what the Lord had called me to do. And I did. It didn't happen the way I planned, though.

For the first three days of the Miss America Scholarship Pageant, the fifty-one contestants stayed at the Walt Disney World Resort in the tropical city of Orlando, Florida. It was a time of fun, meeting other state title-holders, going to various lunches, speaking with the press, and hearing from the Miss America board and directors about the upcoming events in Atlantic City, New Jersey. On a bright sunny Florida afternoon we had an important meeting with a director of the Miss America program. He walked into the room with a smile on his face, and all of us young women clapped for him as he took the podium to speak. I don't remember much of what he said that day, but I got the impression that he wasn't looking for a Christian Miss American that year. Basically, He reminded us that when dealing with the media we should be as politically correct as possible, keeping our Christian beliefs to ourselves.

I sat there a bit stunned and my heart sank. I thought, "Why am I here?" Not only was I singing a gospel song for my talent, but my community service issue was part of Focus on The Family, a very outspoken Christian organization. I recalled that many former Miss America Pageant winners were strong, bold, super models for Christ. I thought we were supposed to be ourselves?

It wasn't for me to understand. I made a commitment in my heart to not water down my faith during my private interview with the judges, as well as to belt out my song "His Eye Is On The Sparrow" with all of my heart! If becoming Miss America meant that I had to compromise what I knew was right, I didn't want to win. As I have told God in the past, "I don't want it if it's not from you, Lord!"

I gave my best, believing that I could win. I have no regrets. I didn't come that far to fail and I believed that I was the best person for the job of Miss America that year. However, I didn't become Miss America 1998… Kate, Miss Illinois, was named Miss America that year. She *was* politically correct and her role model for AIDS research was the liberal actress Sharon Stone. Kate advocated passing out condoms in public schools and stood openly for gay and lesbian rights. She and I are quite opposites. However, many changes took place for the Miss America Organization throughout that following year. They took on new leadership and Nicole Johnson, a woman not ashamed of the gospel of Christ, was crowned Miss America 1999. I am reminded again sister, that what we do for our Father is never in vain.

> *"Therefore dear brothers, stand firm. Let nothing move you. Always give yourselves fully to the work of the Lord, because you know that your labor in him is not in vain."*
> 1 Corinthians 15:58

When my name wasn't announced the final night of the Miss America Pageant, I felt peace. I didn't understand God's plans at the time, but later I realized that my dream had come true by his will and not my own. My dream was so much bigger than having the title of Miss America. My dream was to speak to young people all over our country about striving for excellence in their lives. My dream was also to be a light in the dark places where the crown would take me that I might not otherwise be invited. I believe that God was giving me what was *best* for me, even if I didn't realize it at the time. As a dear friend reminded me, "Sheri, we should still dream, we should still work hard and pray even harder, but when things fall apart we have to remember that we are the ones who are fallible, not our Leader. And we can rest in his grace, because even though we can't see the way, he knows exactly where we're going."

When I flew back to my home state of Iowa, I began to realize that I had a new focus. I saw that dreams don't always come true the way we plan. Don't you think that when Cinderella escaped to the ball, she wanted her future story to begin with her Prince Charming that evening? She probably didn't want to run off at midnight, back to a life of slavery to her stepmother and wicked stepsisters. But her dream came true in a different way than she expected. It took a glass slipper and a determined Prince, but she got her fairytale ending.

A new dream had begun for me, too. Sure, there were moments when tears welled up in my eyes because I didn't win Miss America. I felt like I had let my wonderful Miss Iowa Pageant Board down, people I had grown to love and respect. I also felt like I had let my supportive family and friends down. But in my spirit I felt joy, knowing that God was still in control. I hadn't let him down. He comforted me, showing me his grace. He opened hundreds of doors for me to share his love and light in this dark world as I traveled across Iowa and beyond. I praised him for placing me exactly where he wanted me to be. Even now, several years later, doors open just because of the dream that God had placed in a little girl's heart.

> "So here's what I want you to do, God helping you: Take your everyday, ordinary life – your sleeping, eating, going to work, and walking around life – and place it before God as an offering. Embracing what God does for you is the best thing you can do for him…"
>
> *Romans 12:1 and 2 The Message*

Dreamers are the people who change the world! Did you know that the United States of America would have never existed if someone hadn't had a dream to be free from religious persecution in Europe? Have you ever thought that African Americans would still be in bondage to slavery if our President Abraham Lincoln hadn't had a dream to see them as a free people? What about something as simple as the light bulb or the microwave? Those things all began to take shape with a dream in someone's heart. In fact, this book I'm writing is one of my dreams. I want to see it in your hands, adding blessings to your life!

Amber Harrington is a vivacious twelve-year-old girl. She has a bright smile on her face and a twinkle in her eye. She loves swimming and playing the piano. I received an email from her yesterday in which she shared her dream of being a singer. I smile as I think about her dream. I know that if she commits to practicing her vocal lessons often, gives up some playtime, and doesn't listen to the "negative nay-sayers," she can achieve that dream. It might not be on as grand a scale as someone like Celine Dion or Michael W. Smith, but then again, it might be.

Did you know that Michael Jordan was cut from his high school basketball team? Look at him today. He will go down in our history books as one of the greatest basketball players that ever lived. What if he would have given up his dream? The Chicago Bulls certainly wouldn't have won as many championships.

Have you watched any of the Rocky movies with Sylvester Stalone? I must say that I'm not a boxing fan, but my husband, dad and brother enjoy all five of his movies. So I have seen them. My favorite is movie number four, when Rocky fights against the giant Russian named Drago. Before Rocky leaves America to train in Russia for the big fight, he sits down with his young son to have a talk. He tells him, "When you're hurting, if you go the extra round, that will make all the difference in your life." I believe that's true. As young women our dreams aren't always easy to achieve. It's never giving up, though, that makes all the difference in our lives.

Don't lose sight of where you're headed

A super model is a dreamer. Our main dream is to be like Christ. I love how the Message Bible records Hebrews 12,

> "Keep your eyes on Jesus, who both began and finished this race we're in. Study how he did it. Because he never lost sight of where he was headed - that exhilarating finish in and with God - he could put up with anything along the way: cross, shame, whatever. And now he's there, in that place

> of honor right along side God. When you feel yourself flagging in your faith, go over the story again, item by item, that long litany of hostility he plowed through. That will shoot adrenaline into your souls!"

During Jesus' time on earth he finished his immediate goal of conquering death so you and I may have life. His dreams for his years here were established. He never lost sight of where he was going! He went through *it all* and never gave up! I know that he is standing beside us, sister, saying, "You can do it, too! I gave you my Spirit and you can do all things through me."

One of my mentors, Reed DeVries, is a funny youth pastor. At a conference he challenged the audience to make a list of 100 dreams. At first I thought, "How hard can this be, Reed?" Later when I sat down with my purple pen and notebook, I realized that it would be much harder than I thought. The first thirty dreams were pretty simple to come up with. They were things that I have always dreamed about. I wrote dreams like having three or four children, traveling across Europe, writing books, owning a Jaguar convertible, giving money to missions, spending Christmas with my family in New York City, and taking my mom and grandma for a week-long vacation at a spa. After those thirty dreams were down on paper, my mind went blank. I couldn't believe that it was happening to me. I had always been a dreamer and had always asked God to open my eyes to dream more, to dream bigger. I started praying. I asked the Lord to remind me of what a big God he is. I may be a little girl, but I have great big Daddy!

Over the next couple of days I started to add to that list of thirty dreams. I eventually did write down 100. I realized that God wants me to do things with my life that I could only do through him. He wants me to have and see things that are only possible with him. The Bible says,

> "Delight yourself in the Lord and he will give you the desires of your heart."
> PSALM 37:4

Satan used Joseph's brothers to imprison him. Satan wants to use fear, self-fulfilling prophesy, and our own mediocre thought to imprison us. He doesn't want us to remember that our Father wants to give us our dreams. Our Father wants his girls to have the desires of our hearts. He loves us, sister.

Chase your dreams

What would you do if you knew you couldn't fail? Would you try out for that part in the school play? Would you talk to your parents about spending a summer on the mission fields of South America? Would you take that leap and apply for the college or that scholarship that you think you will never get? Would you volunteer next summer to work with children who have special needs? Would you be like Rudy Ruddiger, in his biographical movie *RUDY*, and go to football practice every day at the University of Notre Dame, never playing in one single game, until the last game of your senior year? He believed that he could be more than his friends and relatives told him he could be. He was determined to win.

You may have a parent who tells you that you will never amount to anything. Or, you may have a teacher who has labeled you a failure. As Les Brown, one of my favorite communicators says, "Someone's opinion of you does not have to become your reality!" I want you to know that a negative parent and a misdirected teacher should not affect the reality God wants you to live!

Les also said that the wealthiest place on the planet is the cemetery, because there we find all the ideas that were never acted upon, all the dreams that people dared not to reach because they were afraid of failure. Have your dreams died, dear super model? Ask the Holy Spirit to bring them back to life.

I don't know about you, but my Bible clearly tells me that I can do all things through Christ. His opinion of me is all that matters. Knowing that Jesus believes in me shoots adrenaline into my soul! I know he created me for greatness – what am I doing with his creation? What are you doing?

Each day that you and I wake up is a day to start all over again.

> "Because of the Lord's great love we are not consumed, for his compassions never fail. They are new every morning; great is your faithfulness."
>
> *Lamentations 3:22 and 23*

I love what red-haired Anne says in *Anne of Green Gables*, "Tomorrow is fresh with no mistakes in it!" Yes, each day is a chance to start all over again. We may have given up on our dreams the day before, but we can rekindle those flames in the morning. One of my dad's close friends, Jerry Meadows, says, "Today is the first day of the rest of your life!" If we have 10,000 days left on this earth or just 100, it is still the first day of the rest of our lives. We choose how it is going to play out. No matter where we live or who our parents are, our dreams from our Father are our dreams to reach. No one can stop us from reaching our dreams but ourselves.

Do you think Paul was never afraid to tell someone about Christ? Sure he was. He may have been bold and full of the Holy Spirit's power, but he was still an imperfect man like you and me. He knew that his dream and calling to share the gospel throughout the Roman world would only come about if he faced his fears and trusted the Lord. What if he had decided to give up when he and Silas were thrown in prison in Philippi? He would have never made it to Thessalonica (or Europe) and you and I might still be lost souls today.

He said,

> "However, I consider my life worth nothing to me, if only I may finish the race and complete the task the Lord Jesus has given me - the task of testifying to the gospel of God's grace."
>
> Acts 20:24

My dear sister, I pray for you to be like Paul, that you may finish the race and complete the tasks the Lord Jesus has given you. He will provide you with everything you need to finish the race: a track to run on, the light of his Word to guide your steps, water from the Spirit to quench your thirst, and a finish line to celebrate in the end. Your job is to go! Go and dream the dreams that he has placed before you! Never give up, never say, "I can't," and never forget that Jesus is running with you every step of the way!

Keep believing
There are those who say it can't be done -
That your dreams are too big and your hopes too high,
They must not know the size of the God you serve.
Keep believing

Let's Start Living!

After running several miles, your track coach finally says it's time to go home. You collapse on the ground, thrilled to take off your running shoes. Your body is fatigued and sweat is dripping off your forehead. All you can think about is that cold, sparkling glass of water your mom will hand you when you reach the doorstep of your house.

Today is different, though. Your mom does hand you a glass, but it's filled with mud and grass. You push past her, thinking your mom is playing a truly sick joke. Feeling exhausted, you run to the kitchen sink to find a clean glass. Today all the glasses are dirty though. Filthy! There is not a clean dish in the house and mold is running rampant. Your body thrashes, sweat continues to pour, and your head throbs with pain. There is no water to be found, only dirt leaking from the faucets.

I believe God gave me that vision especially for us, sister. I believe he feels that way about you and me at times. As he looks down on his creation all he sees is dirt. He is looking for just one glass, just one young woman who is pure. He is searching for just one young woman who longs to be filled with the refreshing water of his mercy. If only we would ask for forgiveness. If only we would desire holiness. God wants to fill us up. Why do we willingly remain dirty?

> *"So roll up your sleeves, put your mind in gear, be totally ready to receive the gift that's coming when Jesus arrives. Don't lazily slip back into those old grooves of evil, doing just what you feel like doing. You didn't know any better then; you do now. As obedient children, let yourselves be pulled into a way of life shaped by God's life, a life energetic and blazing with holiness. God said, 'I am holy; you be holy!'"*
>
> 1 Peter 1:13-16 The Message

Ron Luce, President of Teen Mania Ministries, challenges us this way, "It's time for us to quit acting like babies and quit wetting out pants. It's normal for babies to wet their pants, but when they're three, four and five years old, something is wrong! Yet we have so many Christians who are just like that. They have grown up. They've been in church a long time, but they are not mature Christians. They're still wetting their pants; that is, they're still walking in sin. They're still letting fire extinguishers put their fire (for God) out. They have had it re-lit time and time again, yet the same thing continues to extinguish the fire. They keep messing themselves. They keep dirtying up their life with garbage, sin, compromise, and mediocrity, acting like it's cute. When babies mess their pants for the first time, their parents think it's cute. It's not cute anymore when you're ten or twelve years old and still messing your pants. It's time to grow up. It's time to mature."

I couldn't agree more! I am preaching to myself. By sitting around, going to dozens of filthy movies, hanging out at the mall with lukewarm friends, listening to garbage music, playing the dating game, and half-heartedly going to church on Sundays, we are shutting our ears to God's call on our lives. We need to grow up in our walks with Christ. We need to quit making excuses, pick up the armor of God and never look back!

This journey we have shared together is only the beginning. It's time for the tests, sister. Don't worry, I'm not going to quiz you on what you have read or learned. Now that you have commitment to be a super model of Christ, Satan knows about your new life and is going to do all he can to stop you. This very moment is the time to put on the full armor of God. Stand strong!

> *"Finally, be strong in the Lord and in his mighty power. Put on the full armor of God so that you can take your stand against the devil's schemes. For our struggle is not against flesh and blood, but against the rulers, against the authorities, against the powers of this dark world and against the spiritual forces of evil in the heavenly realms. Therefore put on the full armor of God, so that when the day of evil comes, you may be*

> *able to stand your ground, and after you have done everything, to stand. Stand firm, then with the belt of truth buckled around your waist, with the breastplate of righteousness in place, and with your feet fitted with the readiness that comes from the gospel of peace. In addition to all this, take up the shield of faith, with which you can extinguish all the flaming arrows of the evil one. Take the helmet of salvation and the sword of the Spirit, which is the word of God."*
>
> EPHESIANS 6:10-17

Those verses explain why God has given us the armor and what it's for. It's right at our fingertips. All we have to do now is put it on. Pick it up. Let's get going! God is ready to do a new thing in our hearts! He has greater things in store for us!

> "Forget the former things; do not dwell on the past. See, I am doing a new thing!"
>
> *ISAIAH 43:18 AND 19A*

You and I are going to be blown away by the blessings God has prepared for us because of our obedience. He will use your life and mine to change this world. We are world-changers. And our future is going to be greater than our past.

We agree that beauty on the inside goes much deeper than the junk we see on TV and in secular magazines, right? The short-term glories we may achieve on earth are meaningless compared to a life lived for our Lord. With his armor on we are ready to march into battle, unafraid and fully prepared.

When my husband Tony enlisted in the U.S. Military, he took on a new life. When he was sworn in, he took upon himself a new duty, a new calling. He made a commitment to new leadership, to new training, and to a new mission. As super models we must do the same. When we accepted Christ as our Savior, our lives took a new direction. Our whole world changed. *Now* we must commit to his leadership, put ourselves under his training and take up our new mission—the cross. There is no looking back, no faltering along the trail. We are in a spiritual battle, with our armor on and our torches blazing high above our heads!

With that in mind, no matter what we see tomorrow while walking down the hall at school, we must remember our new calling. As we watch movies this weekend with our friends, we must remember our new leadership. As we wrestle with wanting to look and act like the world around us, we must remember the cross. It's our new mission.

> "If you are pleased with me, teach me your ways so I may know you."
>
> *Exodus 33:13*

Real love

As super models, our beauty is pure and will last a lifetime. It isn't based on breast implants, botox skin injections, and liposuction. Nor is it based on wearing designer labels, having perfectly applied make-up, or being doused in name brand perfume. Yes, we will continue to see our female peers using all their feminine wiles to attract the attention of young men. And it will work at first. With God's armor on, we should remember that kind of attention is short-lived and shallow. We don't need it! We can be sure that the next bouncy brunette with big blue eyes and a tight T-shirt will send the male eyes shooting the opposite direction in an instant. That's not true love. That's not even true admiration. It's certainly not true respect. True love and real beauty are something that has stood the test of time.

I have seen that true love while visiting my grandpa Bob in the nursing home. He gazes with pride at his faithful wife, Ethel. Sure, her skin is wrinkly and there is gray in her hair. However, to him she is more beautiful today than she was fifty-five years ago. They made a commitment that has stood the test of time. That real beauty has lasted through good times and bad times. It's remained through rich times and poor times, through sickness and health. You see, the beauty my grandfather sees comes from a servant's heart, an unconditional love for her husband, and a steady relationship with Christ. That love is *rare* and *real*. That love makes a romance based on looks and sex completely vanish.

Each day you and I must choose whom we will model our lives after. Will we choose to be like the models that strut their stuff on the false runways of life? Or will we choose to walk as young women of God on the true highway that leads to life? We are rare and priceless to our Father. He created us with a divine purpose in mind. Are you going to answer the call? Are you ready to mature, to grow in your walk with Christ?

Will you choose life?

I once heard a story that begins on a cold winter day in communist Russia. A group of Christians met together for worship. They could not meet in a church building or out in the open like you and I do. Their evil dictator opposed any mention of God or Jesus. Anyone caught reading a Bible was imprisoned or killed. Although the believers were well aware that their punishment might be death, the message of Christ could not be quenched. These people were hungry, as each day salvation came to dozens of men, women, and children.

One clear afternoon a secret meeting had begun in a small farmhouse. On one wall was a faded print of Jesus. The Word of God was opened as believers began to fellowship in the Spirit.

A loud bang interrupted the scene as three armed guards entered the house. The guards' faces were expressionless, yet hatred shone through their eyes. A quiet hush came over the Christians as terror filled their hearts and chills ran down their spines. The women grabbed their children, huddling in corners. Fear gripped the men like a tight leather glove. One of the guards noticed the faded print of Jesus hanging on the wall. He tore it down. Gripping it in his right hand, he yelled, "Get up! All of you! You must march past this picture of your so-called Savior, spit in his face, curse his name, and walk out those doors. If you do not, we will kill you one by one. Did you hear me? Do you want to die today?"

Silence lingered. Sweat and tears dripped down the faces of the believers. Could they stand firm? Would they be willing die for Christ? How could they let their children die? Was it worth giving up everything? It all came down to a choice between this world and temporary happiness or the next world and eternal joy. Their blood would be spilt, suffering with their Savior. But what about their children's blood? Their friends' blood?

Again the guard shouted his ultimatum! A tall man moved first, taking the hand of his wife, looking into her desperate eyes. He spit on his Savior's face, cursed his name, and watched as his family did the same, escaping through the doors. One by one the other believers, in their fear, did the same. Women were weeping, their children screaming.

There was one person left. The guards stood in shock as a six-year-old little girl walked up to the picture of Jesus. She pulled it up into her arms. Her tiny hand moved lovingly as she wiped off the spit from his face. With courage unknown to common men, she held the picture to her chest. Looking the men in the eyes she said, "Shoot me."

The Holy Spirit came upon the three guards instantly. They began to weep aloud as they went out the doors and shot all 39 of the people who denied their "so-called" Savior that day.

A small girl had more courage and faith than dozens of adults had. She had a faith that would rather die for her Lord than live a life without him. What about you? Will you live for him? Will you live each day wanting to know him so badly that you would give up everything, for just a second in his presence? *"For me, to live is Christ and to die is gain."* Philippians 1:21

You and I may never be faced with death as a result of our faith. We are free to have a Bible in our home or go to church on Sunday morning. We are safe and for the most part we are free. So Jesus may not be asking us to die for him, but I believe he is asking us to *live* for him. He asks us not just to go through the motions of being a Christian, but to pour our lives into loving him, into serving him, into knowing him. He asks us to abandon our fears, turn to the guards of this world, and say, "Shoot me. I would rather live my life as a model of and for Christ than choose any of the temporary thrills this life may offer."

Mountains and valleys

I recently received an email from a teenage friend of mine. She seems to have it all together. She is tall and pretty. She is a leader in her youth group and daily strives to be a super model of Christ. Struggling, she writes, "For the longest time I am constantly dealing with my weight. I seem to feel like I will never be thin enough. So since I was around 15 years old I constantly struggle with eating and not wanting to eat. It has never gotten out of hand though, but not a day goes by that I don't feel fat. I am constantly thinking of how I am going to loose more weight. There were times when I would eat things that I knew that I shouldn't have eaten. I remember putting my fingers down my throat, ready to make myself purge. But, I never could go through with it. I knew that if I did it once I would probably never be able to stop. Sometimes I'd make it a game like lets see if I can eat less today than I did yesterday. I really don't know why being skinny is so important to me? I think it is more of being able to control part of my life, feeling insignificant too. It is something that you can pray for me to overcome."

After reading this book, are you still facing a similar situation, wrestling with your flesh? It might not be with food, but with your self-image, with your parents, with what people think about you, with how much money you have, or with an addiction. Do you have situations in your life that feel like mountains in front of you?

There have been mornings I have wanted to pull the sheets up over my head and let the day pass by. Pain is real and being a follower of Christ doesn't make it all disappear. As I look back at those days of feeling like I was at the bottom of a deep valley (and I know there will be more ahead), I am humbled to see the miracles God had in store for me. There are some things we won't know until we get to heaven, but other things we can see as if God's hand was painting a canvas right before our eyes.

When I was fifteen I went with my youth group to "Rock The Planet" in Colorado. It was a large retreat in the summer with hundreds of teens from across the U.S. The speakers and musicians were anointed. I know the Lord changed me while at that conference. But the time he changed me the most was not in a crowded auditorium.

On a free afternoon our group took a ride up to Rocky Mountain National Park, where we had time to explore. We ran along the trails and up to a high peak that was covered in cold, white snow in mid-July. I took some time to sit on the mountainside by myself. I ran my fingers across the frozen blades of grass, fixing my eyes on the view in front of me. It took my breath away. The beauty and vibrant colors went on as far as my eyes could see. The magnitude of how vast, towering, and mighty my God must be hit me deep in my soul. His whisper taught me that he allows us to go through the valleys to prepare our hearts for those astounding mountaintop moments. He wants us to have those days that fill our spirits up and remind us that our Daddy loves us and is in complete control of our lives. He gives us days where we stand in awe of who he is and of all he has done for us. Then he allows us to grow as we face the valleys, knowing that he will never let us go. He will give us the strength to *overcome*! By his Word and his Spirit we are overcoming!

A Super Model's life

The movie *Princess Diaries* is adorable. I love watching young Mia turn from a shy and invisible teenager into the true Princess of Genovia. She thought that she was just an ordinary, even below average, fifteen-year-old girl. But she was royal by birth. She had a choice to make. Whether she accepted the role and responsibilities of becoming a princess or not, she was still, in fact, a princess. She couldn't change who she really was, but she could choose to ignore her calling and run! (Sounds a lot like God's royal daughters, huh?) To say the least, Mia was afraid and had every intention of running. It was much easier not to change. It was easier to take the wide gate.

Right before she ran something vital and monumental happened. She opened a diary that her father meant to give her for her sixteenth birthday. Enclosed was a powerful letter that he had hoped would encourage her to accept the person she was created to be. Here is what he told her:

> "Courage is not the absence of fear, but rather the judgment that something else is more important than fear.
>
> The brave may not live forever, but the cautious do not live at all.
>
> From now on you'll be traveling the road between who you think you are and who you can be.
>
> The key is to allow yourself to make the journey."

His powerful words echoed in Mia's mind and heart as she made the decision to accept her role as princess. She got out of her "self" and realized that her life meant so much more than she thought it did. She became courageous and brave while traveling the new road to whom she was going to become.

As super models, you and I are on a journey too. Our Father has given us the keys to the journey and the assurance that we will make it through. He has written us a letter to hide in our hearts as we grow from who we are into who we can be.

Who you are right now is not a reflection of who you can be tomorrow. Leave behind the past and things that have held you back. It's time to take the next step on the journey toward becoming that model of Christ that you were made to be. You, dear super model, are ready for the challenge. You are fearfully and wonderfully made for such a time as this! The question of *How to be a Super Model* has been partly answered, but the rest of the answer is between you and your heavenly Daddy. The key, is to allow him to take you on the journey.

To order additional copies of

How to be a Super Model

call toll-free

1-866-297-2820

or order online at

www.sheriprescott.com